Published in the United States by

An Imprint of Precept®
PO Box 182218
Chattanooga, TN 37422

ISBN 978-1-63687-155-4

First edition, January 2024
Printed in the United States of America

Where we
are going

Let's look ahead to where we are going. Below are the passages of Scripture we will be studying together to give us a full picture of faith and work.

Purpose

Eternal Significance in Everyday Work

FAITHFUL LIVING, PART TWO

yarrow

An Imprint of Precept®

Chattanooga

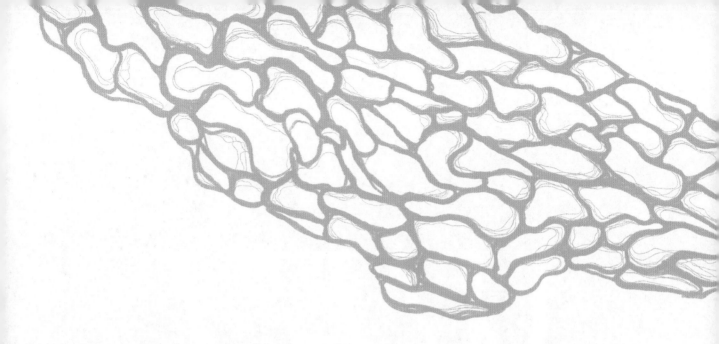

WEL-COME

What do you want to be when you grow up?

We are asked this question as early as we can remember.

In elementary school, we drew pictures of ourselves as teachers, singers, doctors, firefighters, and astronauts, dreaming about what we might become one day. In high school, we took aptitude tests that tried to answer the question for us. As we entered college or the workforce, the stress kicked in as the pressure to find an answer intensified.

And then, before we knew it, we've chosen a major, forged a career path, and begun our journey while still trying to figure it all out along the way. And although the question changes, it remains. Every time we meet someone new, one of the first questions they ask will undoubtedly be:

What do you do?

And underneath it all, we continue to ask ourselves a million more questions . . .

What do I want to do with my life?
Does what I do matter?
What am I good at?
What are my dreams?
What is God calling me to do?
Does God care what career I choose?
How do I honor Him with my work?

Throughout our lives, from childhood into adulthood, we are fascinated by these questions of work, career, and purpose. And rightly so. On average, we spend about 90,000 hours or *ten straight years* of our lives working. And for many of us, it's probably more.

As such, our study of faithful living needs to include a conversation about faith and work. The goal of *Purpose: Eternal Significance in Everyday Work* is to learn how to live faithfully through the work that is before us.

As Christians, we are called to be disciples of Jesus in every moment and every area of our lives. What if we sensed the same peace going into the office Monday morning as going to church on Sunday? What if we felt the presence of God in our weekly team meetings at work as we did while meeting with our discipleship groups? What if our mundane day-to-day tasks are as holy as our daily Scripture reading?

Whether you are in your dream job or a job you dread . . . whether you have known what you were meant to do from the age of four or if you are still figuring it out . . . whether you are searching for a new job, self-employed, a full-time parent, an unpaid volunteer, or a full-time student—the work you have been called to and the work before you is important, good, and holy. And this study is for you.

WELCOME TO YARROW!

View a welcome video from one of our Yarrow team members by scanning this QR Code.

Where we've **been**

If you are joining us from Part One of our Faithful Living Study, welcome! God is ready to meet you here and continue the work He began in you.

If you are new to this Faithful Living study, welcome to you too! We invite you to complete Part One of our Faithful Living Study, *Sojourn: Flourishing on Earth, Yearning for Heaven*. Doing so will help you cultivate a deeper understanding of what it means to live as a faithful exile here on earth. But if you would like to jump in here, that's great too. We are glad to have you!

Let's begin by reviewing what we mean by *faithful living* to ensure we start on the same page.

Faithful living is more than a to-do list of behaviors and tasks to add to our lives. We are talking about a complete change of perspective—a change of heart. Faithful living is seeing this world through the eyes of God and adopting His perspective. We remember our future heavenly home and our position as exiles here on this earth, which will change the way we live, think, act, love, and, especially for this study—*work*, here and now. *It is a new way of living.*

If you still have questions, we hope you'll bring them. And we encourage you to open your heart and mind to all that God speaks to you through Scripture.

We pray that your time in the Bible will pull you deeper into God's presence and enable you to grow in Christ. We also pray that it will lead to lasting heart change, affecting the way you live and work, from the inside out.

What to **expect**

The old saying goes, "If you give a man a fish, you feed him for a day. If you teach a man to fish, you feed him for a lifetime." In other words, it's more important to know *how* to get a meal in the long run than to have one in hand today.

The Bible works the same way. Instead of giving you exact instructions for every circumstance, God gave you the Bible with big-picture truths about humanity, life, and Himself. The answers you seek aren't found in step-by-step instructions, but in knowing God. As your relationship with Him grows, so does your ability to see the world and your life through His eyes.

John talks about this in his Gospel:

Abide in me, and I in you. As the branch cannot bear fruit by itself, unless it abides in the vine, neither can you, unless you abide in me. I am the vine; you are the branches. Whoever abides in me and I in him, he it is that bears much fruit, for apart from me you can do nothing.

John 15:4–5

WHAT TO EXPECT

Scan the QR code to watch a video where we further explain what you can expect from this study.

The goal of this Bible study is not to give you a fish but to teach you how to fish. Basically, don't expect to be told what to believe. As we guide you through Scripture, you will develop the skills needed to approach the Bible on your own. We will leave room for you to take away what God has planned specifically for you.

Growing up in school, we focused on grades and scores, sometimes at the expense of authentic learning. We often bring that mindset to Bible studies. Here at Yarrow, we do Bible studies a little differently than you might be used to. We camp out in a passage for a while to let God speak through Scripture to our hearts and minds.

The questions we ask will not usually have a right or wrong answer. This might feel unfamiliar to you, and that's okay. This journey is designed to get you thinking critically about the text, the world, and your personal experiences. Studying this way allows us to absorb what the Holy Spirit is teaching us. Take your time. We'll help you make the connections, but it will be important that you rely on the Holy Spirit to guide you as well—not just us.

Throughout this study, we will go to Nehemiah, Genesis, Exodus, 1 Corinthians, and Colossians to discover how to live faithfully *through the work we do here and now.*

How it **works**

Feel free to adapt it to your life, schedule, and relationships. Here's all we ask:

1.

Choose two believers to talk to. We've seen that genuine transformation and growth often involve other people. Whether you're stumped, frustrated, or delighted by what you're discovering, it's important to have others walking with you. If you're meeting with a group, those people are automatically built in. If you're studying on your own, we encourage you to share with a believing spouse, friend, or mentor along the way.

2.

Aim for consistency. Building routines that prioritize time in Scripture is an important part of setting yourself up for success. We encourage you to pick a time and place to go to the Bible every day, and then be flexible. If something happens and you miss a day (or a week), don't give up! This journey is about growth, not perfection.

The **Method**

We believe in a hands-on approach to Bible study. The Bible is thousands of years old, and it's easy to skim over strange stories or familiar verses without true understanding. To help you explore Scripture for yourself, we rely on the Precept Bible Study Method:

Observe: What does the text say?

Interpret: What does the text mean?

Apply: How should the meaning affect my life?

Taken together, these three components help you slow down, discover meaning, and find connections to your daily life.

01.

Observe

The key to good observation is to slow down. This component in the process can feel a little tedious, but it's vital. Before you can jump to interpreting or applying Scripture, you must understand what is taking place in the text. Observation exercises will help bring clarity. The most common exercises include:

ANSWER THE 5WS AND AN H:

You'll answer straightforward questions like *who, what, when, where, why,* and *how* using what you read in a particular section of text. For example, you'll answer *when* with time phrases within the text like "the next day" or "in the morning." You'll find clues to *why* questions with words like "therefore" and "because" that explain more about what was just said. Doing this exercise helps you slow down and note the details of what you're reading so you don't miss anything. No special knowledge or insight is required.

MARKING:

To *mark* a word or phrase, you'll visually distinguish it with a shape or color. Once marked, you'll see at a glance where and how often the word or phrase appears. It's best to mark consistently and distinctively; that is, always mark the same word the same way and mark it differently than other words. Marking may also include making notes in the margins on comparisons, contrasts, or terms of conclusion. Marking may seem arbitrary at the moment, but it will help you pick up on themes and important points the author wants you to catch.

LISTING:

To *list* is to record all the details about something or someone in one place. These facts answer the 5Ws and an H questions. Then, you can review and reflect on everything you discover about a topic. This is most helpful when there is a lot of information scattered across several verses or chapters (for example, the miracles of Jesus or the story of creation).

02. Interpret

Once you're clear on what is being said in a text, you then need to know what it means. Thorough and careful observation flows into accurate interpretation. When you interpret Scripture, the context must be considered.

Scripture is a beautiful tapestry. When we observe a text (as outlined above), we focus on a small piece of the larger tapestry. We must also pay attention to the weave binding the material together. The context weaves throughout the entire biblical tapestry and binds it together.

To discover the context, we will pay attention to the historical and cultural context, the surrounding verses, the theme and structure of the entire book, other passages throughout the Bible on the same topic, and the overall story of redemption in Scripture. We may use the tools of cross-references or limited word studies to explore the meaning of a text. We'll ask you to look for key ideas or think about the meaning behind stories, parables, and poems. For example, it's one thing to know what Jesus said in a parable but another to understand what He meant.

Sometimes interpreting is straightforward with an obvious answer. Other times, it is more nuanced. Remember, we aren't going to tell you what to believe, so be patient with yourself. The Bible requires lifelong study, and the more you explore and meditate on Scripture, the more your understanding will grow.

03.

Once you've seen what a text says and understood what it means, you need to consider how it affects your daily life. Sometimes a text will apply directly to something you can do or change externally, and sometimes it applies to matters of the heart or mind (and often, both)! We'll guide you with questions like:

- *What would change in your life if_____were true?*

- *How is your perspective on [current issue] affected by what you just read?*

- *What steps can you take this week to_____?*

Without application, Bible study is little more than an interesting academic exercise. This is where it's most important to have someone else involved. Christians need other Christians, and you'll find that your experience is richer and more enjoyable if you involve someone else in what you're learning.

01. Observe

02. Interpret

03. Apply

THE METHOD

Scan the QR code to learn more about our Bible study method.

---

journal your thoughts

Spend a few moments reflecting on your work, including some of your feelings or questions about it.

1. How do you answer when people ask, *What do you do?*

2. How do you feel about the work you are currently doing?

3. If you could do anything, what would it be?

4. What questions do you still have for God surrounding your work?

Write your thoughts and questions on the following pages.

Go to God *in Prayer.*

Father in heaven,

Creator of work and all good things,

I thank You . . .

First and foremost, for Your presence,

For being near me now as I prepare to embark on this journey.

I invite You along, O Father,

As I seek to understand Your plan for work and Your plan for me.

Search my heart,

Search my dreams,

Search my deepest desires,

And align them all with Yours, Your will, and Your call over my life.

I surrender all things to You.

Open my eyes, O God, to the moving of Your Spirit.

Open my ears, O God, to hear Your voice.

Open my heart, O God, to be fully Yours.

You have my trust.

You have my love.

Amen.

Self- Reflection *#1*

Let's begin by identifying your beliefs on faith and work. The following statements are meant to help you pause and reflect on some of these beliefs. Respond to each one as honestly as possible, remembering that it's okay to be exactly where you are. As we work through this study, we will return to these and see if, and how, your perspectives may be changing along the way.

Self-Reflection #1

Circle the phrase that describes what you believe about each statement below.

1. Work was a part of God's original design for humans.

Strongly Disagree   Disagree   Neither Disagree nor Agree   Agree   Strongly Agree

2. God has uniquely gifted me.

Strongly Disagree   Disagree   Neither Disagree nor Agree   Agree   Strongly Agree

3. I know the gifts with which God has gifted me.

Strongly Disagree   Disagree   Neither Disagree nor Agree   Agree   Strongly Agree

4. God has placed a unique purpose and calling over my life.

Strongly Disagree   Disagree   Neither Disagree nor Agree   Agree   Strongly Agree

5. I know the unique purpose and calling that God has placed over my life.

Strongly Disagree   Disagree   Neither Disagree nor Agree   Agree   Strongly Agree

6. I am living out God's calling over my life.

Strongly Disagree   Disagree   Neither Disagree nor Agree   Agree   Strongly Agree

7. I am happy in the work I am currently doing.

Strongly Disagree   Disagree   Neither Disagree nor Agree   Agree   Strongly Agree

8. My work is one of the primary ways that I praise and glorify the Lord.

Strongly Disagree   Disagree   Neither Disagree nor Agree   Agree   Strongly Agree

9. My work is one of the primary ways that I love and serve others.

Strongly Disagree   Disagree   Neither Disagree nor Agree   Agree   Strongly Agree

10. Rest is an important part of my weekly rhythm.

Strongly Disagree   Disagree   Neither Disagree nor Agree   Agree   Strongly Agree

journal your thoughts

Take a moment to reflect on your answers on the previous page.

1. Did any of these questions stir up an emotion or response?

2. Were you surprised by any of your answers?

3. What other questions do you have for God as you begin this study?

Write your thoughts and questions here.

Go to God *in Prayer.*

Use your reflections above to write a prayer to God. Tell Him what is on your heart, your questions, and the dreams that are stirring up in you. Write out your prayer to Him in the space provided. Tell Him the truth, confess when you have disobeyed, ask Him for what you need, and invite Him into your Bible study over these next few weeks.

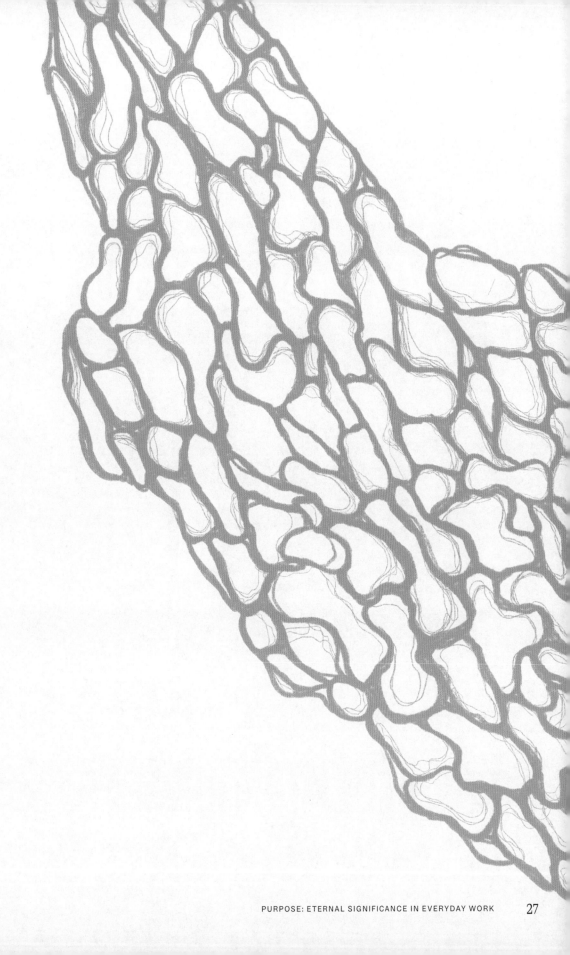

CHAPTER TWO

Where You Are

Nehemiah 1

We will explore the book of Nehemiah throughout this Faithful Living series to see examples of people adopting God's perspective. As we read the first two chapters of Nehemiah, we will focus on a different emphasis within the text than in *Sojourn,* Part One of our series. We believe that Scripture is living and active, and as such, new insights can be gained from rereading the same Scripture.

CONTEXT

Nehemiah is a historical book of the Old Testament. The events took place after the Babylonians destroyed Jerusalem and its temple and had taken many of the Jewish people into exile. At this point in the story, some of the Jewish people had begun to return to Jerusalem to rebuild both their city and their culture. They had successfully rebuilt the temple, but as we will read in Nehemiah 1, the city walls were still in ruins, a source of great trouble and shame for the Israelites.

Scan the QR code to learn more about the context of the book of Nehemiah.

Let's begin with Nehemiah 1.

As you read Nehemiah 1, pay special attention to Nehemiah, the man. Take note of any phrase describing him—where he is, what he is doing, and how he feels.

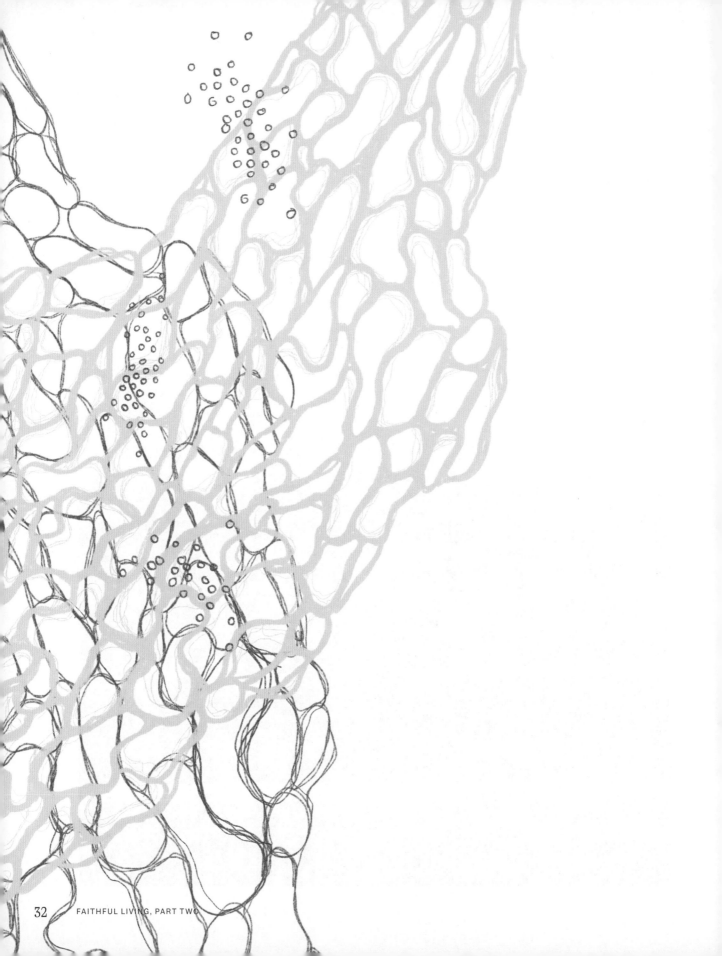

Nehemiah 1

1   The words of Nehemiah the son of Hacaliah. Now it happened in the month of Chislev, in the twentieth year, as I was in Susa the citadel,

2   that Hanani, one of my brothers, came with certain men from Judah. And I asked them concerning the Jews who escaped, who had survived the exile, and concerning Jerusalem.

3   And they said to me, "The remnant there in the province who had survived the exile is in great trouble and shame. The wall of Jerusalem is broken down, and its gates are destroyed by fire."

4   As soon as I heard these words I sat down and wept and mourned for days, and I continued fasting and praying before the God of heaven.

5   And I said, "O LORD God of heaven, the great and awesome God who keeps covenant and steadfast love with those who love him and keep his commandments,

6   let your ear be attentive and your eyes open, to hear the prayer of your servant that I now pray before you day and night for the people of Israel your servants, confessing the sins of the people of Israel, which we have sinned against you. Even I and my father's house have sinned.

7   We have acted very corruptly against you and have not kept the commandments, the statutes, and the rules that you commanded your servant Moses.

8   Remember the word that you commanded your servant Moses, saying, 'If you are unfaithful, I will scatter you among the peoples,

9   but if you return to me and keep my commandments and do them, though your outcasts are in the uttermost parts of heaven, from there I will gather them and bring them to the place that I have chosen, to make my name dwell there.'

10   They are your servants and your people, whom you have redeemed by your great power and by your strong hand.

11   O Lord, let your ear be attentive to the prayer of your servant, and to the prayer of your servants who delight to fear your name, and give success to your servant today, and grant him mercy in the sight of this man."
Now I was cupbearer to the king.

1.
―――――――――――――――――――――――――――――

List any initial observations about Nehemiah below.

2.
―――――――――――――――――――――――――――――

What news does Nehemiah receive about his people in verse 3?

3.
―――――――――――――――――――――――――――――

How do we see Nehemiah responding to this news, beginning in verse 4 and continuing throughout the rest of the chapter?

4.

What does this show us about Nehemiah's heart and what is important to him?

5.

Prayer is an overflow of our heart and its deepest desires. What request to God does Nehemiah's prayer culminate with in verse 11?

6.

Who is Nehemiah referring to as *this man* in verse 11?
(Look to the next sentence to help you.)

7.
_____

What is Nehemiah's job/role in verse 11?

8.
_____

Why do you think the author may have included Nehemiah's job here?
Why might it be significant?
*Note: We will get more information on this question in the next session with chapter 2.
This is meant to get you thinking.*

WHAT IS A CUPBEARER?

A cupbearer was a high-ranking official of the king's court whose primary responsibility was serving wine to the king and the royal table.

Because of the risk of poisoning to the king, the cupbearer often had to guard the king's wine, sometimes even tasting it before it was served to the king.

As such, he was a person who had proven himself trustworthy and loyal to the king.

Reflect and apply.

So far, we have observed and interpreted the text of Nehemiah 1. Now, let's move to application and ask how this text can impact our lives. Take your time with these questions—reflecting and praying through each one.

1.

What are some burdens or passions that God has placed on your heart?
Maybe it's a particular burden, like Nehemiah's for his people and the wall of Jerusalem. Or perhaps it's a special dream or goal. What breaks your heart? What makes you excited? If nothing comes to mind right away, spend time with God in prayer and ask Him.

2.

Where has God placed you?
We will learn more about Nehemiah's position as the king's cupbearer in the next chapter, but for now, know that God placed him there for a purpose. Think about the places God has placed you—in your family, work, neighborhood, and your larger community.

3.

How might these things be connected?
How might the positions where God has you and the desires or burdens He has placed on your heart be connected?

Go to God *in Prayer.*

Before we finish our time in Nehemiah 1, take a moment to thank God for the Bible and everything you've discovered today. Write a prayer to God thanking Him for what He has revealed to you about your own heart, where He has placed you, and any connections you've seen. Share with Him what new things are stirring inside you and what new questions you may have. Write your prayer to Him in the space provided.

CHAPTER THREE

In the Waiting

Nehemiah 2

Let's continue from where we left Nehemiah in our last session. God had placed him in the position of the king's cupbearer. God also heavily burdened Nehemiah's heart for the people and the city of Jerusalem. Let's read chapter 2 to learn how God connects these two aspects of Nehemiah's life.

Let's read Nehemiah 2.

As you read Nehemiah 2, mark any mention of *God* in your text with a triangle or highlight it with a specific color.

Here is our marking suggestion:

"So I prayed to the God of heaven."

Nehemiah 2

1   In the month of Nisan, in the twentieth year of King Artaxerxes, when wine was before him, I took up the wine and gave it to the king. Now I had not been sad in his presence.

2   And the king said to me, "Why is your face sad, seeing you are not sick? This is nothing but sadness of the heart." Then I was very much afraid.

3   I said to the king, "Let the king live forever! Why should not my face be sad, when the city, the place of my fathers' graves, lies in ruins, and its gates have been destroyed by fire?"

4   Then the king said to me, "What are you requesting?" So I prayed to the God of heaven.

5   And I said to the king, "If it pleases the king, and if your servant has found favor in your sight, that you send me to Judah, to the city of my fathers' graves, that I may rebuild it."

6   And the king said to me (the queen sitting beside him), "How long will you be gone, and when will you return?" So it pleased the king to send me when I had given him a time.

7   And I said to the king, "If it pleases the king, let letters be given me to the governors of the province Beyond the River, that they may let me pass through until I come to Judah,

8   and a letter to Asaph, the keeper of the king's forest, that he may give me timber to make beams for the gates of the fortress of the temple, and for the wall of the city, and for the house that I shall occupy." And the king granted me what I asked, for the good hand of my God was upon me.

9   Then I came to the governors of the province Beyond the River and gave them the king's letters. Now the king had sent with me officers of the army and horsemen.

10 But when Sanballat the Horonite and Tobiah the Ammonite servant heard this, it displeased them greatly that someone had come to seek the welfare of the people of Israel.

11   So I went to Jerusalem and was there three days.

12   Then I arose in the night, I and a few men with me. And I told no one what my God had put into my heart to do for Jerusalem. There was no animal with me but the one on which I rode.

13   I went out by night by the Valley Gate to the Dragon Spring and to the Dung Gate, and I inspected the walls of Jerusalem that were broken down and its gates that had been destroyed by fire.

14   Then I went on to the Fountain Gate and to the King's Pool, but there was no room for the animal that was under me to pass.

15   Then I went up in the night by the valley and inspected the wall, and I turned back and entered by the Valley Gate, and so returned.

16   And the officials did not know where I had gone or what I was doing, and I had not yet told the Jews, the priests, the nobles, the officials, and the rest who were to do the work.

17   Then I said to them, "You see the trouble we are in, how Jerusalem lies in ruins with its gates burned. Come, let us build the wall of Jerusalem, that we may no longer suffer derision."

18   And I told them of the hand of my God that had been upon me for good, and also of the words that the king had spoken to me. And they said, "Let us rise up and build." So they strengthened their hands for the good work.

19   But when Sanballat the Horonite and Tobiah the Ammonite servant and Geshem the Arab heard of it, they jeered at us and despised us and said, "What is this thing that you are doing? Are you rebelling against the king?"

20   Then I replied to them, "The God of heaven will make us prosper, and we his servants will arise and build, but you have no portion or right or claim in Jerusalem."

Let's begin with observation.

1. _____

Reviewing where you marked *God* in the text, how do you see God using the position in which He placed Nehemiah to fulfill the purpose He had for Nehemiah?

2. _____

What do we learn about God's role in Nehemiah's plans?

3. _____

Look at verse 2:1. When does this part of Nehemiah's story take place?

4. ───────────────────────────────────────

Look back to verse 1:1. When did Nehemiah first receive the news concerning Jerusalem?

5. ───────────────────────────────────────

The Jewish calendar is made up of 12 months. Chislev is the ninth month, and Nisan is the first. How long was it between the time Nehemiah first heard about Jerusalem until God gave him the opportunity to act on it?

6.

Based on what we have read of Nehemiah's story in chapters 1 and 2, what do you suppose Nehemiah may have been doing during those months of waiting? What verses give you that idea?

7.

Are you in a time of waiting regarding your work? If so, in what ways?
Perhaps you are waiting for a job you love, to finish a degree, an opportunity to pursue your heart's dream, or something else.

8.

Following Nehemiah's example, how can you continue to live faithfully and glorify the Lord in your work exactly where you are, even as you may be waiting on Him?

Go to God *in Prayer.*

As we conclude our time in Nehemiah, let's pause and pray. Thank the Lord for where He has placed you, even if it is not where you wish to be. Share with God the things you are waiting on and the deepest desires of your heart. And then, take a moment to surrender those dreams and plans back to Him. Ask Him to open your heart to His will as you continue this journey. Write your prayer to Him in the space provided.

CHAPTER FOUR

Summary

Nehemiah 1–2

Spend time slowing down and reflecting on all you have discovered from Nehemiah 1–2 by filling out the chart on the next page. Review previous sessions and all that God has revealed to you.

If you are unable to answer some questions today, that's okay. We will practice this at the end of each passage of Scripture. A question that is hard to answer today may become clearer as you go. At the end of the study, we will look at all the charts together to see the Bible as one full story and how our own stories intersect with God's story.

Theme/Big Idea

What did you learn about God/Jesus?

What did you learn about yourself?

What did you learn about work?

What did you learn about faithful living?

Personal Takeaway

Go to God *in Prayer.*

You'll find these summary sessions are shorter than a typical session. Use the extra time and space you have today to sit with the Lord. Thank Him for all He has taught you and has begun to stir up in you throughout your study of Nehemiah 1 and 2. Tell Him what is on your heart and ask Him any questions that may still be on your mind. Write your prayer to Him in the space provided.

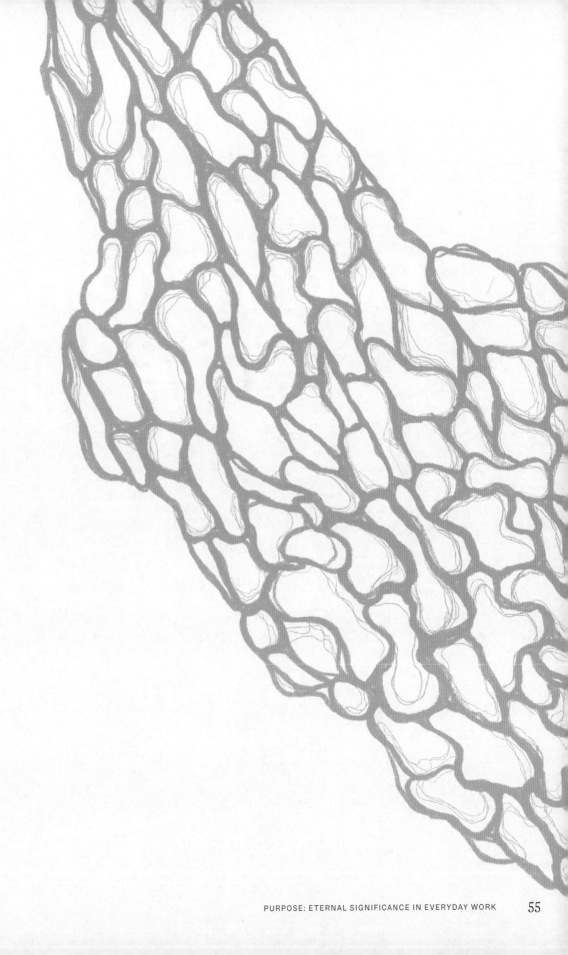

CHAPTER FIVE

God's Original Design

Genesis 1–2

Now that we have spent time in Nehemiah's story learning from his faithful example, let's go back to the beginning of humanity to explore God's original design for humans and work.

THE BIBLE IS ONE STORY

Scan the QR code to learn more about the Bible being one single narrative that points to Jesus.

Let's read Genesis 1–2.

As you read, pay special attention to God's actions each day, as well as His mandates for Adam and Eve.

Genesis 1

1 In the beginning, God created the heavens and the earth.

2 The earth was without form and void, and darkness was over the face of the deep. And the Spirit of God was hovering over the face of the waters.

3 And God said, "Let there be light," and there was light.

4 And God saw that the light was good. And God separated the light from the darkness.

5 God called the light Day, and the darkness he called Night. And there was evening and there was morning, the first day.

6 And God said, "Let there be an expanse in the midst of the waters, and let it separate the waters from the waters."

7 And God made the expanse and separated the waters that were under the expanse from the waters that were above the expanse. And it was so.

8 And God called the expanse Heaven. And there was evening and there was morning, the second day.

9 And God said, "Let the waters under the heavens be gathered together into one place, and let the dry land appear." And it was so.

10 God called the dry land Earth, and the waters that were gathered together he called Seas. And God saw that it was good.

11 And God said, "Let the earth sprout vegetation, plants yielding seed, and fruit trees bearing fruit in which is their seed, each according to its kind, on the earth." And it was so.

12 The earth brought forth vegetation, plants yielding seed according to their own kinds, and trees bearing fruit in which is their seed, each according to its kind. And God saw that it was good.

13 And there was evening and there was morning, the third day.

14 And God said, "Let there be lights in the expanse of the heavens to separate the day from the night. And let them be for signs and for seasons, and for days and years,

15 and let them be lights in the expanse of the heavens to give light upon the earth." And it was so.

16 And God made the two great lights—the greater light to rule the day and the lesser light to rule the night—and the stars.

17 And God set them in the expanse of the heavens to give light on the earth,

18 to rule over the day and over the night, and to separate the light from the darkness. And God saw that it was good.

19 And there was evening and there was morning, the fourth day.

20 And God said, "Let the waters swarm with swarms of living creatures, and let birds fly above the earth across the expanse of the heavens."

21 So God created the great sea creatures and every living creature that moves, with which the waters swarm, according to their kinds, and every winged bird according to its kind. And God saw that it was good.

22 And God blessed them, saying, "Be fruitful and multiply and fill the waters in the seas, and let birds multiply on the earth."

23 And there was evening and there was morning, the fifth day.

24 And God said, "Let the earth bring forth living creatures according to their kinds—livestock and creeping things and beasts of the earth according to their kinds." And it was so.

25 And God made the beasts of the earth according to their kinds and the livestock according to their kinds, and everything that creeps on the ground according to its kind. And God saw that it was good.

26 Then God said, "Let us make man in our image, after our likeness. And let
    them have dominion over the fish of the sea and over the birds of the
    heavens and over the livestock and over all the earth and over every
    creeping thing that creeps on the earth."

27   So God created man in his own image,
            in the image of God he created him;
            male and female he created them.

28 And God blessed them. And God said to them, "Be fruitful and multiply and
    fill the earth and subdue it, and have dominion over the fish of the sea
    and over the birds of the heavens and over every living thing that moves on
    the earth."

29 And God said, "Behold, I have given you every plant yielding seed that is on
    the face of all the earth, and every tree with seed in its fruit. You shall have
    them for food.

30 And to every beast of the earth and to every bird of the heavens and to
    everything that creeps on the earth, everything that has the breath of life, I
    have given every green plant for food." And it was so.

31 And God saw everything that he had made, and behold, it was very good.
    And there was evening and there was morning, the sixth day.

Genesis 2

1   Thus the heavens and the earth were finished, and all the host of them.

2   And on the seventh day God finished his work that he had done, and he rested on the seventh day from all his work that he had done.

3   So God blessed the seventh day and made it holy, because on it God rested from all his work that he had done in creation.

4   These are the generations
> of the heavens and the earth when they were created,
> > in the day that the LORD God made the earth and the heavens.

5   When no bush of the field was yet in the land and no small plant of the field had yet sprung up—for the LORD God had not caused it to rain on the land, and there was no man to work the ground,

6   and a mist was going up from the land and was watering the whole face of the ground—

7   then the LORD God formed the man of dust from the ground and breathed into his nostrils the breath of life, and the man became a living creature.

8   And the LORD God planted a garden in Eden, in the east, and there he put the man whom he had formed.

9   And out of the ground the LORD God made to spring up every tree that is pleasant to the sight and good for food. The tree of life was in the midst of the garden, and the tree of the knowledge of good and evil.

10   A river flowed out of Eden to water the garden, and there it divided and became four rivers.

11   The name of the first is the Pishon. It is the one that flowed around the whole land of Havilah, where there is gold.

12   And the gold of that land is good; bdellium and onyx stone are there.

13   The name of the second river is the Gihon. It is the one that flowed around the whole land of Cush.

14   And the name of the third river is the Tigris, which flows east of Assyria. And the fourth river is the Euphrates.

15 The LORD God took the man and put him in the garden of Eden to work it and keep it.

16 And the LORD God commanded the man, saying, "You may surely eat of every tree of the garden,

17 but of the tree of the knowledge of good and evil you shall not eat, for in the day that you eat of it you shall surely die."

18 Then the LORD God said, "It is not good that the man should be alone; I will make him a helper fit for him."

19 Now out of the ground the LORD God had formed every beast of the field and every bird of the heavens and brought them to the man to see what he would call them. And whatever the man called every living creature, that was its name.

20 The man gave names to all livestock and to the birds of the heavens and to every beast of the field. But for Adam there was not found a helper fit for him.

21 So the LORD God caused a deep sleep to fall upon the man, and while he slept took one of his ribs and closed up its place with flesh.

22 And the rib that the LORD God had taken from the man he made into a woman and brought her to the man.

23 Then the man said,

> "This at last is bone of my bones
>   and flesh of my flesh;
>   she shall be called Woman,
>   because she was taken out of Man."

24 Therefore a man shall leave his father and his mother and hold fast to his wife, and they shall become one flesh.

25 And the man and his wife were both naked and were not ashamed.

1. ───────────────────────────────

What do we see God doing throughout days 1–6?
Note: You can look to Genesis 2:2 to see how the Bible describes what God is doing.

2. ───────────────────────────────

In these chapters, we see God as a creative and working God. Because verse 27 tells us that we were all created in the image of God, what does this tell you about yourself?

3. ───────────────────────────────

List God's plan/command for humankind from each of the following verses below.

- 1:26

- 1:28

- 2:15

4.

Based on these verses, what was God's original design for humankind?
Note: This was before the Fall in Genesis 3 and was always a part of God's plan for us.

5.

Look back to 1:28. What is God doing as He gives them this mandate?

6.

How does this impact your understanding of the purpose for work? How do you see faith relating to work?

7.

How does this impact the way you see your own work?

8.

In what ways do you see your work as a continuation of God's mandate in the garden? How do you see your work as a partnership and co-laboring with God?

If this question feels hard to answer, think about how you are stewarding God's creation and gifts, whether that be His land, His people, or even the talents and resources He has given you personally. Think about the ways you are joining in His creativity or striving for excellence in the work He has given you to do.

So God created man **in his own image.**

GENESIS 1:27

Go to God *in Prayer.*

Let's take a moment to come before God. What insights did God give you about work, and more specifically, about your own work? Thank God for the beautiful plan He has called us all to and for the special purpose He has given to you through your responsibilities. Commit your work to Him today. Write your prayer to Him in the space provided.

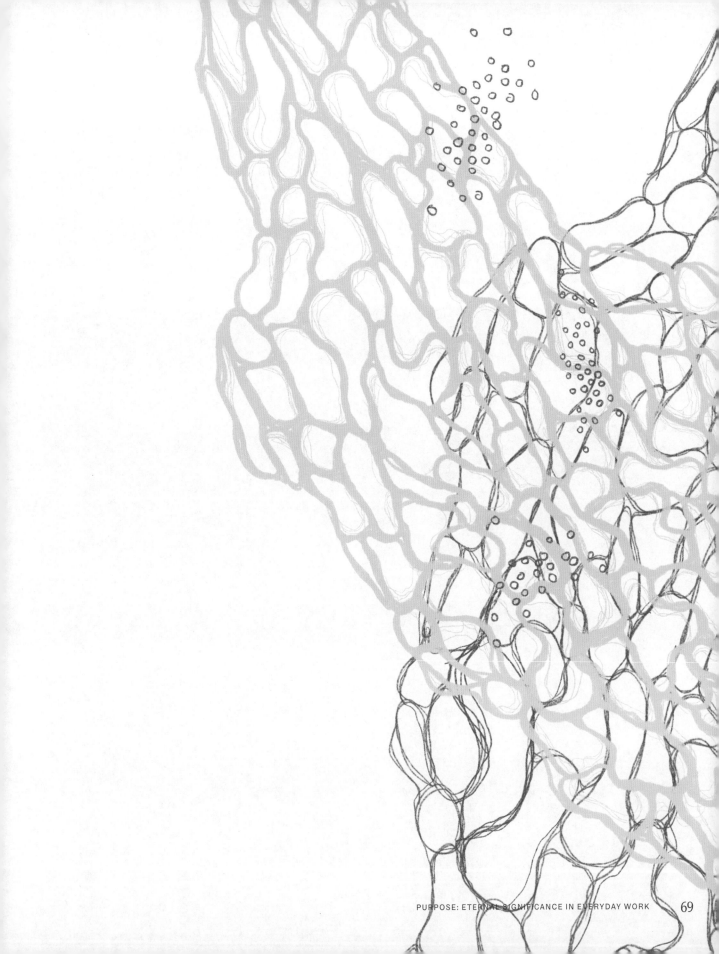

CHAPTER SIX

Rest and Sabbath

Genesis 2

> In our conversation about work, we'll discuss God's original design for rest and Sabbath. If this is a new concept for you, don't worry. We'll walk through this together, exploring Scripture to discover God's example and teaching about rest and Sabbath.

Let's return to Genesis 2.

Look at Genesis 2:2–3 and mark each of the following distinctively:

- *Who?* Mark *God* and His pronouns with a triangle.

- *What?* Mark any indicators of what God is doing, like *finished*, by underlining them.

- *When?* Look for any time markers, like *the seventh day*, and circle them.

Here are some marking suggestions:

1. "...God finished his work that he had done..."

2. "...and he rested"

3. "And on the seventh day..."

Genesis 2

2   And on the seventh day God finished his work that he had done, and he
    rested on the seventh day from all his work that he had done.

3   So God blessed the seventh day and made it holy, because on it God rested
    from all his work that he had done in creation.

72   FAITHFUL LIVING, PART TWO

1. ─────────────────────────────

What do you see God doing on/to the seventh day? List them below.

2. ─────────────────────────────

What do we see God modeling for us in these verses?

3. ─────────────────────────────

From what you know and have learned about God, why do you think God, who is almighty and all-powerful, would choose to rest on the seventh day?
Note: Once again, this was before the Fall. It was not simply a response to the Fall and the curse (more on that tomorrow). Rest was always a part of God's plan.

4. ─────────────────────────────

Knowing God blessed this day and made it holy, what is His desire for our attitude and approach towards rest?

Let's read Exodus 20:8–11.

Here, we will learn more about God's invitation regarding rest and Sabbath. For context, we are entering the story as God gives Moses the Ten Commandments on Mount Sinai after the Israelites have exited from Egypt. As we will see, Sabbath was a command in the Old Testament, but its purpose was often misunderstood. When Jesus came, He reminded us of the true meaning and gift behind the Sabbath. Jesus personally participated in the practice of Sabbath while on earth. As such, Sabbath is not meant to be a legalistic practice, and it remains a valuable and wise invitation from God for us today.

SABBATH

If Sabbath is a new concept to you, we invite you to scan the QR code for additional background and context.

Exodus 20

8   "Remember the Sabbath day, to keep it holy.

9   Six days you shall labor, and do all your work,

10 but the seventh day is a Sabbath to the LORD your God. On it you shall not do any work, you, or your son, or your daughter, your male servant, or your female servant, or your livestock, or the sojourner who is within your gates.

11 For in six days the LORD made heaven and earth, the sea, and all that is in them, and rested on the seventh day. Therefore the LORD blessed the Sabbath day and made it holy.

Reflect and apply.

1.

How do these verses relate to what we read in Genesis?

2.

In your own words, what was God's commandment to the Israelites? And how is this still God's invitation for us today?

3.

Underline the word *"for"* in verse 11. This word helps us to answer the question of *why.* Why did God command the Israelites to remember the Sabbath and keep it holy?

4.

If you responded to God's invitation to rest/Sabbath, how would this impact your life? How would this impact your faithfulness in your work?

5.

What fears or challenges do you foresee in taking rest/Sabbath? How can you work to overcome them?

Maybe you feel like you can't afford a day off, or a day without productivity sends a shiver down your spine. Perhaps you have no idea how you will fill an entire day with rest. These fears and challenges are legitimate, but God offers us something worth pursuing. Be honest with God. Start exactly where you are and keep practicing.

6.

We have a gift that the ancient Israelites did not—living in light of Jesus and all He has done for us. How does remembering this affect the way you view rest and the challenges you mentioned above?

Go to God *in Prayer.*

We'll return to rest and Sabbath in the next session and create a plan to practice this in our own lives. Let's take a moment to pray. Thank God for the grace and kindness He shows us in His invitation to rest and Sabbath. Ask Him for help where you need it and invite Him into this practice. Write your prayer to Him below.

CHAPTER SEVEN

Live the Sabbath

Genesis 2

Sabbath is a *practice.* And as such, it takes intentionality. We'll create a plan for *when* and *how* you can begin to practice Sabbath.

My Sabbath Plan

First, choose a day of the week to rest from work and spend the day in worship, rest, and celebration. (It doesn't have to be Sunday!)

Then, think through options for how you would like to spend your day. Sabbath isn't necessarily about doing less but about doing things that bring refreshment, healing, and wholeness to our bodies and spirits. Try to be detailed in your plan. Think beyond sleeping in or taking a nap when it comes to rest, although this can certainly be a part. If you have a family or young children, you may need to be creative! But we encourage you to think and pray through ways to invite them to practice the Sabbath alongside you. Use the questions below to guide you:

- **How can you worship the Lord on this day?**
  Maybe by going to church, spending extra time in prayer, reading your Bible or a spiritual book, taking a prayer walk, listening to worship music, or serving someone in need.

- **What activities feel like rest to you?**
  Maybe it is moving your body, slowing down to cook a meal, reading, working with your hands, or a hobby.

- **What activities will bring life and joy to your day?**
  Maybe sharing a good meal with friends, visiting family, or spending time in nature.

- **What activities (besides work) would you like to rest from on this day?**
  Maybe social media or technology altogether, shopping, or spending.

My Sabbath Plan

Day of the Week:

PLAN:

Morning:

Afternoon:

Evening:

Things I will rest from:

Go to God *in Prayer.*

We will continue into Genesis 3 in the next session. We will read about the Fall and the curse and how they affected both work and rest. Now, let's take a moment to pray. Ask God for His grace to help you practice Sabbath and overcome any lingering fears or challenges. Invite Him into your practice of rest. Share with Him how you hope it impacts you personally, your life, and your work. Write your prayer to God in the space provided.

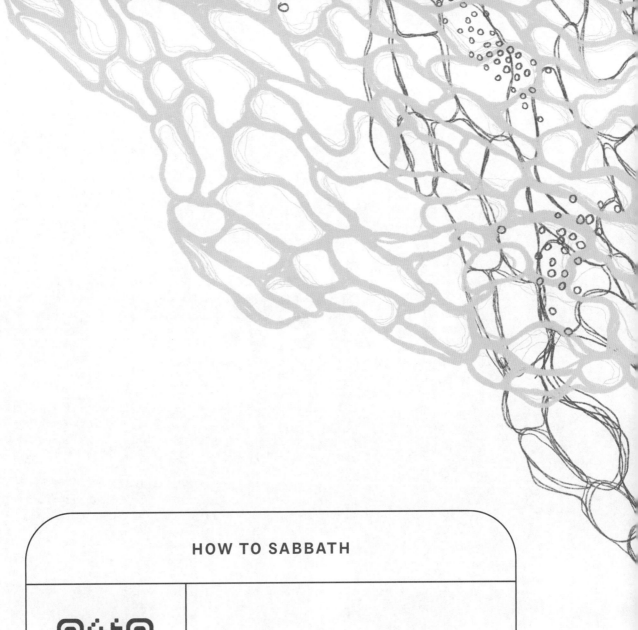

HOW TO SABBATH

Scan the QR code to discover more about how these truths apply to your life.

CHAPTER EIGHT

Cursed Is the Ground

Genesis 3

While work was a beautiful part of God's original design for humankind, we'll read in this chapter how sin invaded that original design and affects us still today.

Read through Genesis 3.

As you read Genesis 3, keep in mind God's original design for humans and work and His original mandates to humankind that we read in Genesis 1 and 2.

Genesis 3

1   Now the serpent was more crafty than any other beast of the field that the LORD God had made. He said to the woman, "Did God actually say, 'You shall not eat of any tree in the garden'?"

2   And the woman said to the serpent, "We may eat of the fruit of the trees in the garden,

3   but God said, 'You shall not eat of the fruit of the tree that is in the midst of the garden, neither shall you touch it, lest you die.'"

4   But the serpent said to the woman, "You will not surely die.

5   For God knows that when you eat of it your eyes will be opened, and you will be like God, knowing good and evil."

6   So when the woman saw that the tree was good for food, and that it was a delight to the eyes, and that the tree was to be desired to make one wise, she took of its fruit and ate, and she also gave some to her husband who was with her, and he ate.

7   Then the eyes of both were opened, and they knew that they were naked. And they sewed fig leaves together and made themselves loincloths.

8   And they heard the sound of the LORD God walking in the garden in the cool of the day, and the man and his wife hid themselves from the presence of the LORD God among the trees of the garden.

9   But the LORD God called to the man and said to him, "Where are you?"

10 And he said, "I heard the sound of you in the garden, and I was afraid, because I was naked, and I hid myself."

11 He said, "Who told you that you were naked? Have you eaten of the tree of which I commanded you not to eat?"

12 The man said, "The woman whom you gave to be with me, she gave me fruit of the tree, and I ate."

13 Then the LORD God said to the woman, "What is this that you have done?" The woman said, "The serpent deceived me, and I ate."

14 The LORD God said to the serpent,

> "Because you have done this,
>> cursed are you above all livestock
>> and above all beasts of the field;
> on your belly you shall go,
>> and dust you shall eat
>> all the days of your life.

15 I will put enmity between you and the woman,

>> and between your offspring and her offspring;
> he shall bruise your head,
>> and you shall bruise his heel."

16 To the woman he said,

> "I will surely multiply your pain in childbearing;
>> in pain you shall bring forth children.
> Your desire shall be contrary to your husband,
>> and he shall rule over you."

17 And to Adam he said,

> "Because you have listened to the voice of your wife
>> and have eaten of the tree
> of which I commanded you,
>> 'You shall not eat of it,'
> cursed is the ground because of you;
>> in pain you shall eat of it all the days of your life;

18 thorns and thistles it shall bring forth for you;

>> and you shall eat the plants of the field.

19 By the sweat of your face

>> you shall eat bread,
> till you return to the ground,
>> for out of it you were taken;
> for you are dust,
>> and to dust you shall return."

20 The man called his wife's name Eve, because she was the mother of all living.

21 And the LORD God made for Adam and for his wife garments of skins and clothed them.

22 Then the LORD God said, "Behold, the man has become like one of us in knowing good and evil. Now, lest he reach out his hand and take also of the tree of life and eat, and live forever—"

23 therefore the LORD God sent him out from the garden of Eden to work the ground from which he was taken.

24 He drove out the man, and at the east of the garden of Eden he placed the cherubim and a flaming sword that turned every way to guard the way to the tree of life.

1.

Review Genesis 1:26, 28, and 2:15 and remind yourself of God's mandates for Adam. How do we see Adam and Eve straying from these mandates as Genesis 3 unfolds?

Let's look closely at what God says to Adam beginning in verse 17.

2.

In God's words to Adam in verses 17–19, what curses does God pronounce regarding work? List them below.

3.

After Adam and Eve's disobedience, what changed about work?

4. ────────────────────────────────────

In what ways do you see this curse showing up in work today?

5. ────────────────────────────────────

In verse 23, what does God continue to have Adam do even after he is exiled from the garden?

6. ────────────────────────────────────

What does this tell us about God's design for humans and work?

Reflect and apply.

Many challenges and limitations to work still exist today because of sin. What was meant to be a joy-filled way to co-labor and partner with God now comes with mixed emotions. Below are some examples of how sin can invade our work life.

1.

Circle any of the following challenges that you can relate to in your work life. Be honest with yourself and with God, remembering that this is not meant to be a source of guilt or shame—we all face these struggles. The first step to overcoming them is to acknowledge them.

Perfectionism	Finding identity in work	Greed	Difficulty with coworkers/boss
Workaholism	Feeling under appreciated	Comparison	Feeling insignificant in the work you are doing
Fatigue	Dissatisfaction	Burnout	Always chasing down the next thing
Feeling purposeless	Unhealthy work environment	Laziness	Other: _____

2. _____

Reflect on the challenges you circled. Choose 1 or 2 to elaborate on below. How do you see this showing up in your work?

3. _____

Now, for each of the challenges you chose, write one way you can begin to combat it as you pursue faithful living through your work.

For example, regarding difficulty with coworkers/boss: I will seek God's wisdom in my interactions with him/her (as Nehemiah did in 2:4).

Go to God *in Prayer.*

Let's pause and pray as we close out our time in Genesis. Thank God for the gift and blessing of work, particularly your work—no matter where you are. Confess to Him the areas where you have fallen short, and thank Him for the areas that are going well. Ask Him to help you in your journey to return to His original design for work. Write your prayer to Him in the space provided.

Take a step
in community.

After you have reflected and talked with God, take an opportunity to *talk with someone else*. Choose 1–3 people you trust and share with them what you are learning about faith and work. Confess to them the sins and challenges you face in your work, remembering that the Bible encourages our confession of sin to one another.

Therefore, confess your sins to one another and pray for one another, that you may be healed. James 5:16

Share with them the actions you want to take to return to God's original design. Ask them to check in and hold you accountable as they walk the rest of this journey with you. Remember that community is about vulnerability and accountability. If this feels new, scary, or hard, that's okay. We encourage you to take the risk.

Not sure what to say? You can start like this:

I've been working through a Bible study on faith and work and learning about God's original design for work. I'm finding that I'm struggling with some things regarding my own work, like_____,_____, and_____. But I would like to overcome these challenges and make my way back to God's original design in these ways:_____.

Would you be willing to walk with me, pray for me, and hold me accountable as I try to make these changes?

Self-Reflection #2

Spend time slowing down and reflecting on all you have discovered from Genesis 1–3 by filling out the chart on the next page. Review previous sessions and all that God has revealed to you.

If you are unable to answer some questions today, that's okay. We will practice this at the end of each passage of Scripture. A question that is hard to answer today may become clearer as you go. At the end of the study, we will look at all the charts together to see the Bible as one full story and how our own stories intersect with God's story.

Theme/Big Idea

What did you learn about God/Jesus?

What did you learn about yourself?

What did you learn about rest and work?

What did you learn about faithful living?

Personal Takeaway

Go to God *in Prayer.*

Thank God for all He has taught you throughout your time in Genesis. Share with Him what is on your heart—the things that are exciting, convicting, or confusing you. Be honest with Him. Write your prayer to Him in the space provided.

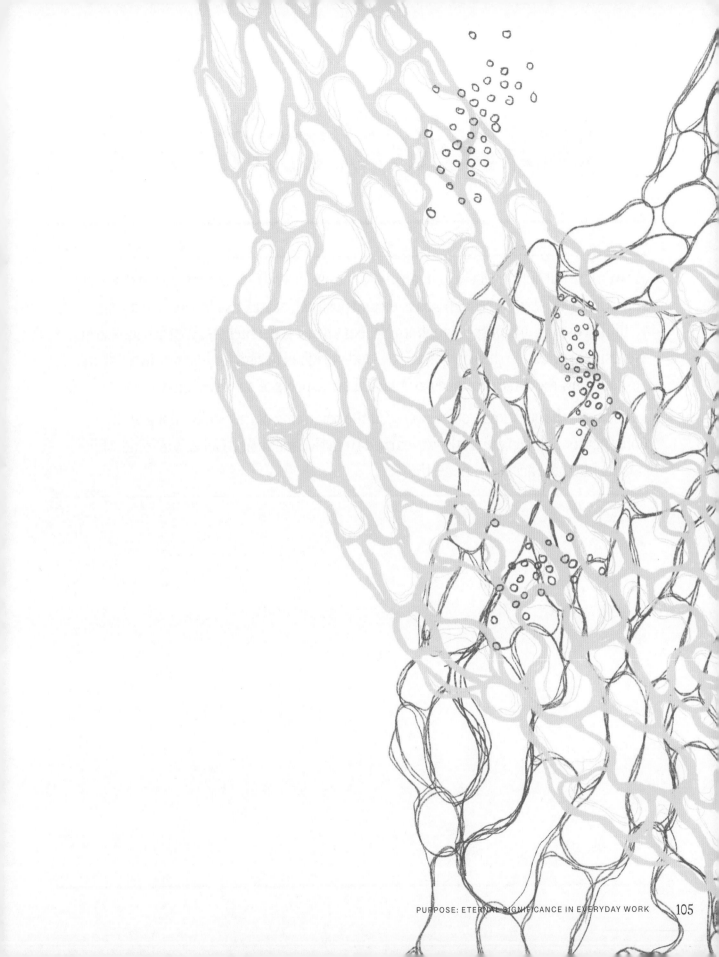

Self-*Reflection #2*

As we close out our time in Nehemiah and Genesis, let's retrace the thread we have been following. God used Nehemiah's passion and position, as well as his time of waiting, to fulfill His plan and purpose for both Nehemiah and the Israelites. We then looked at Genesis to review the theology of work—God's original design for humans in work and rest and how the curse continues to invade these aspects of our lives today.

Let's revisit the questions you answered at the beginning of this study, along with some new ones. Keep the truths we learned from Nehemiah and Genesis in mind while answering these questions honestly.

Self-Reflection #2

Circle the phrase that most closely describes what you believe about each statement below. Along the way, write the references of any relevant verses from Nehemiah or Genesis next to each question, along with any fresh insights or observations.

1. Work was a part of God's original design for humans.

Strongly Disagree   Disagree   Neither Disagree nor Agree   Agree   Strongly Agree

2. God has uniquely gifted me.

Strongly Disagree   Disagree   Neither Disagree nor Agree   Agree   Strongly Agree

3. I know the gifts with which God has gifted me.

Strongly Disagree   Disagree   Neither Disagree nor Agree   Agree   Strongly Agree

4. God has placed a unique purpose and calling over my life.

Strongly Disagree   Disagree   Neither Disagree nor Agree   Agree   Strongly Agree

5. I know the unique purpose and calling that God has placed over my life.

Strongly Disagree   Disagree   Neither Disagree nor Agree   Agree   Strongly Agree

6. I am living out God's calling over my life.

Strongly Disagree   Disagree   Neither Disagree nor Agree   Agree   Strongly Agree

7. I am happy in the work I am currently doing.

Strongly Disagree   Disagree   Neither Disagree nor Agree   Agree   Strongly Agree

8. My work is one of the primary ways that I praise and glorify the Lord.

Strongly Disagree   Disagree   Neither Disagree nor Agree   Agree   Strongly Agree

9. My work is one of the primary ways that I love and serve others.

Strongly Disagree   Disagree   Neither Disagree nor Agree   Agree   Strongly Agree

10. Rest is an important part of my weekly rhythm.

Strongly Disagree   Disagree   Neither Disagree nor Agree   Agree   Strongly Agree

journal your thoughts

Compare your original answers to the questions on the previous page with pages 24-25. Then, reflect on the questions below.

1. Have any of your answers changed? If so, *how* have they changed, and *why*?

2. Are there any areas where you feel a disconnect between the truths of Scripture and what you believe or how you feel? *Please know that these disconnects happen to us all. God's grace helps us on the long journey from head knowledge to heart belief.*

3. What questions do you still have for God as you continue this study?

Journal your thoughts and questions on the following pages.

journal your thoughts

Go to God *in Prayer.*

After you have reflected, take a moment to lay your thoughts out before God. Thank Him and give Him glory for all He is doing in and through you. Ask Him for anything you still hope for as you work your way through the rest of this study. Write out your prayer to God in the space provided. Be honest. Confess whatever is on your heart. Ask Him for what you need and invite Him into this next week of Bible study with you.

CHAPTER TEN

Called by God

Exodus 3:1–4:17

We have explored God's original design for work and how we can begin to return to it despite the challenges. Now, let's apply this on a practical and personal level. In the following sections, we will touch on some common questions that many of us share regarding faith and work. Let's begin by looking at Moses.

CONTEXT

The book of Exodus follows the Hebrews as they depart out of Egypt and journey towards the Promised Land. Moses, a Hebrew-born man raised by the Egyptian pharaoh's daughter, is a central figure in this narrative. Although the Hebrews had been brutally enslaved by the Egyptians, God used Moses to display His great power and glory. Moses confronted pharaoh and led the Hebrews out of Egypt.

Let's begin with observation.

Read Exodus 3:1–4:17 and distinctively mark each of the following:

- *Where?* Look for specific and general locations, like *Horeb* and *a land flowing with milk and honey.* Underline them.

- *God* and His synonyms and pronouns: *Lord, God of your father, he, etc.* Draw a triangle around the word/phrase.

- *Moses* and his pronouns. Draw a circle around the words.

Here are some marking suggestions:

1. "... and came to Horeb, the mountain of God"

2. "God called him out of the bush ..."

3. "And Moses hid his face ..."

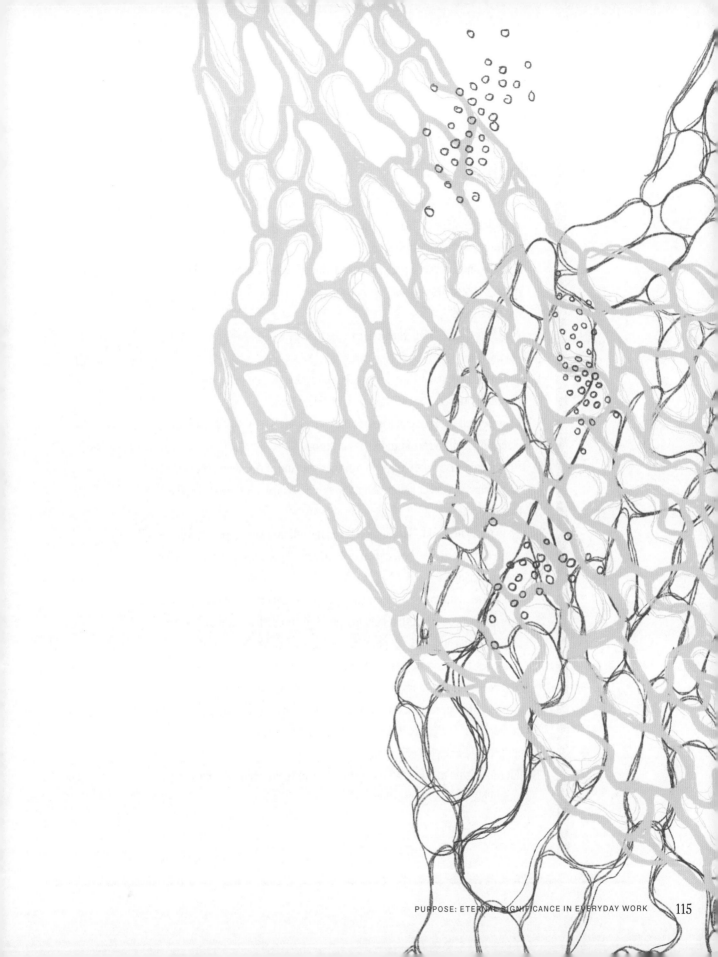

Exodus 3

1   Now Moses was keeping the flock of his father-in-law, Jethro, the priest of Midian, and he led his flock to the west side of the wilderness and came to Horeb, the mountain of God.

2   And the angel of the LORD appeared to him in a flame of fire out of the midst of a bush. He looked, and behold, the bush was burning, yet it was not consumed.

3   And Moses said, "I will turn aside to see this great sight, why the bush is not burned."

4   When the LORD saw that he turned aside to see, God called to him out of the bush, "Moses, Moses!" And he said, "Here I am."

5   Then he said, "Do not come near; take your sandals off your feet, for the place on which you are standing is holy ground."

6   And he said, "I am the God of your father, the God of Abraham, the God of Isaac, and the God of Jacob." And Moses hid his face, for he was afraid to look at God.

7   Then the LORD said, "I have surely seen the affliction of my people who are in Egypt and have heard their cry because of their taskmasters. I know their sufferings,

8   and I have come down to deliver them out of the hand of the Egyptians and to bring them up out of that land to a good and broad land, a land flowing with milk and honey, to the place of the Canaanites, the Hittites, the Amorites, the Perizzites, the Hivites, and the Jebusites.

9   And now, behold, the cry of the people of Israel has come to me, and I have also seen the oppression with which the Egyptians oppress them.

10 Come, I will send you to Pharaoh that you may bring my people, the children of Israel, out of Egypt."

11 But Moses said to God, "Who am I that I should go to Pharaoh and bring the children of Israel out of Egypt?"

12 He said, "But I will be with you, and this shall be the sign for you, that I have sent you: when you have brought the people out of Egypt, you shall serve God on this mountain."

13 Then Moses said to God, "If I come to the people of Israel and say to them, 'The God of your fathers has sent me to you,' and they ask me, 'What is his name?' what shall I say to them?"

14 God said to Moses, "I AM WHO I AM." And he said, "Say this to the people of Israel: 'I AM has sent me to you.'"

15 God also said to Moses, "Say this to the people of Israel: 'The LORD, the God of your fathers, the God of Abraham, the God of Isaac, and the God of Jacob, has sent me to you.' This is my name forever, and thus I am to be remembered throughout all generations.

16 Go and gather the elders of Israel together and say to them, 'The LORD, the God of your fathers, the God of Abraham, of Isaac, and of Jacob, has appeared to me, saying, "I have observed you and what has been done to you in Egypt,

17 and I promise that I will bring you up out of the affliction of Egypt to the land of the Canaanites, the Hittites, the Amorites, the Perizzites, the Hivites, and the Jebusites, a land flowing with milk and honey."'

18 And they will listen to your voice, and you and the elders of Israel shall go to the king of Egypt and say to him, 'The LORD, the God of the Hebrews, has met with us; and now, please let us go a three days' journey into the wilderness, that we may sacrifice to the LORD our God.'

19 But I know that the king of Egypt will not let you go unless compelled by a mighty hand.

20 So I will stretch out my hand and strike Egypt with all the wonders that I will do in it; after that he will let you go.

21 And I will give this people favor in the sight of the Egyptians; and when you go, you shall not go empty,

22 but each woman shall ask of her neighbor, and any woman who lives in her house, for silver and gold jewelry, and for clothing. You shall put them on your sons and on your daughters. So you shall plunder the Egyptians."

Exodus 4

1   Then Moses answered, "But behold, they will not believe me or listen to my voice, for they will say, 'The LORD did not appear to you.'"

2   The LORD said to him, "What is that in your hand?" He said, "A staff."

3   And he said, "Throw it on the ground." So he threw it on the ground, and it became a serpent, and Moses ran from it.

4   But the LORD said to Moses, "Put out your hand and catch it by the tail"— so he put out his hand and caught it, and it became a staff in his hand—

5   "that they may believe that the LORD, the God of their fathers, the God of Abraham, the God of Isaac, and the God of Jacob, has appeared to you."

6   Again, the LORD said to him, "Put your hand inside your cloak." And he put his hand inside his cloak, and when he took it out, behold, his hand was leprous like snow.

7   Then God said, "Put your hand back inside your cloak." So he put his hand back inside his cloak, and when he took it out, behold, it was restored like the rest of his flesh.

8   "If they will not believe you," God said, "or listen to the first sign, they may believe the latter sign.

9   If they will not believe even these two signs or listen to your voice, you shall take some water from the Nile and pour it on the dry ground, and the water that you shall take from the Nile will become blood on the dry ground."

10 But Moses said to the LORD, "Oh, my Lord, I am not eloquent, either in the past or since you have spoken to your servant, but I am slow of speech and of tongue."

11 Then the LORD said to him, "Who has made man's mouth? Who makes him mute, or deaf, or seeing, or blind? Is it not I, the LORD?

12 Now therefore go, and I will be with your mouth and teach you what you shall speak."

13 But he said, "Oh, my Lord, please send someone else."

14 Then the anger of the LORD was kindled against Moses and he said, "Is there not Aaron, your brother, the Levite? I know that he can speak well. Behold, he is coming out to meet you, and when he sees you, he will be glad in his heart.

15   You shall speak to him and put the words in his mouth, and I will be with your mouth and with his mouth and will teach you both what to do.

16   He shall speak for you to the people, and he shall be your mouth, and you shall be as God to him.

17   And take in your hand this staff, with which you shall do the signs."

18   Moses went back to Jethro his father-in-law and said to him, "Please let me go back to my brothers in Egypt to see whether they are still alive." And Jethro said to Moses, "Go in peace."

19   And the LORD said to Moses in Midian, "Go back to Egypt, for all the men who were seeking your life are dead."

20   So Moses took his wife and his sons and had them ride on a donkey, and went back to the land of Egypt. And Moses took the staff of God in his hand.

21   And the LORD said to Moses, "When you go back to Egypt, see that you do before Pharaoh all the miracles that I have put in your power. But I will harden his heart, so that he will not let the people go.

22   Then you shall say to Pharaoh, 'Thus says the LORD, Israel is my firstborn son,

23   and I say to you, "Let my son go that he may serve me." If you refuse to let him go, behold, I will kill your firstborn son.'"

24   At a lodging place on the way the LORD met him and sought to put him to death.

25   Then Zipporah took a flint and cut off her son's foreskin and touched Moses' feet with it and said, "Surely you are a bridegroom of blood to me!"

26   So he let him alone. It was then that she said, "A bridegroom of blood," because of the circumcision.

27   The LORD said to Aaron, "Go into the wilderness to meet Moses." So he went and met him at the mountain of God and kissed him.

28   And Moses told Aaron all the words of the LORD with which he had sent him to speak, and all the signs that he had commanded him to do.

29   Then Moses and Aaron went and gathered together all the elders of the people of Israel.

30 Aaron spoke all the words that the LORD had spoken to Moses and did the signs in the sight of the people.

31 And the people believed; and when they heard that the LORD had visited the people of Israel and that he had seen their affliction, they bowed their heads and worshiped.

Let's focus on Exodus 3:1–10.

These questions will help you slow down and notice details in the text. (We will move deeper into interpretation and application later.)

1. ───────────────────────────────

   Where was Moses when he saw the burning bush? How does the Bible describe this place?

2. ───────────────────────────────

   What was Moses doing there?

3.

In what way did the Lord appear to him?

4.

In verse 4, what does God do to Moses?

5.

Look at verses 7–9. Why is God calling out to Moses?

6.

What does this tell you about the character and heart of God?

7. —————————————————————————

According to God in verse 10, what is Moses' role to be in all of this?

8. —————————————————————————

From this interaction between Moses and God, how would you define a calling or being called by God?

Note: Your calling may not come from an audible voice from God as it did for Moses. It could come in the form of a friend or mentor, a deep-seated passion or dream within you, or in other ways. It is still a calling all the same.

Let's explore our personal callings by looking at two foundational commandments from God for all believers on which our callings can be built.

Read Matthew 28:19–20 and Colossians 3:17.

Matthew 28:19–20

19 Go therefore and make disciples of all nations, baptizing them in the name of the Father and of the Son and of the Holy Spirit,

20 teaching them to observe all that I have commanded you. And behold, I am with you always, to the end of the age."

Colossians 3:17

17 And whatever you do, in word or deed, do everything in the name of the Lord Jesus, giving thanks to God the Father through him.

9.

What is God calling us to do in these verses?

10.

How can you, in your current work and everyday life, respond to these universal calls from God?

Please note: You do not have to be a pastor or ministry worker to make disciples and glorify God with your work. You can do this in every scope of work.

And whatever you do, in word or deed, **do everything in the name of the Lord Jesus,** *giving thanks to God the Father through him.*

Colossians 3:17

Go to God *in Prayer.*

This idea of calling can leave us with more questions than answers. Let's bring all of this before the Lord. Ask God your questions. Share with Him what is stirring in your heart. Thank Him for anything He has revealed or clarified for you today. Invite Him to continue journeying with you. Write your prayer to God in the space provided.

CHAPTER ELEVEN

Explore Your Calling

Exodus 3:1–4:17

Let's explore our personal callings. This idea of calling can sometimes feel ambiguous, mysterious, or confusing. For most of us, it will not come through the audible voice of God in a burning bush like it did for Moses. But perhaps it can be as simple as a desire God has already placed deep inside us— something we can seek out and discover for ourselves.

CALLING

Scan the QR code to discover more about how these truths apply to our lives.

journal your thoughts

Reflect on the questions below, and then use the following pages to journal. These questions will not necessarily lead you to your calling; rather, they will help you to start a conversation with God and your community so that you can continue beyond these pages.

1. What do you love to do? What are you passionate about? What lights you up and gets you excited?

2. What breaks your heart? What is the need around you—in your city, church, country, generation, or world? What is a problem you want to solve?

3. What do you find yourself thinking about all the time? Talking about all the time?

4. What are you good at? What are you not so good at?

5. What opportunities do you presently have? What doors are open? And what doors has God closed?

6. What might God be stirring in your heart? Or is there something you are pushing away (as Moses tried to do)?

7. What was your childhood dream?

8. If you could do *anything,* what would it be?

9. How would you most like to make disciples and glorify God?

journal your thoughts

journal your thoughts

journal your thoughts

Go to God *in Prayer.*

Let's bring all of this before God and lay it at His feet. Thank Him for creating you uniquely and with a purpose. Share with Him what may have come to the surface during your study today—the things stirring in your heart, any questions, or the fears that may exist. Invite Him into this journey of calling, faith, and work with you.

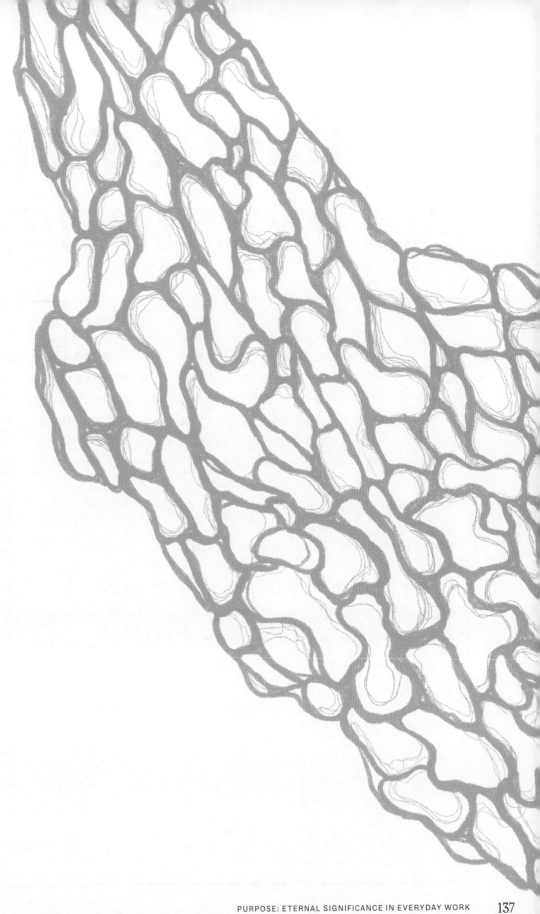

Take a step
in community.

After you have reflected and talked with God, take an opportunity to talk with someone else. Share with a trusted friend or mentor some of your insights and questions about your calling. Ask them to share what they see in you—the talents, the giftings, or the potential callings. Sometimes the people around us can see things we can't.

Not sure what to say? You can start like this:

I've been working through a Bible study on faith and work. Today, I've been reflecting on calling. Here are some things I think may be true about my personal calling:_____.
As someone who knows and loves me, what do you think about this? What are the other things you see in me?

CHAPTER TWELVE

When in Doubt

Exodus 3:1–4:17

In our previous sessions, God called to Moses from the burning bush to lead His people out of Egypt. Today, let's take a closer look at the exchange between God and Moses that follows this initial call.

Beginning in Exodus 3:11, look to where you marked Moses and God on pages 116–120 and follow their exchange. In the chart below, describe each of Moses' oppositions to God in column 2. Then, fill in God's response to Moses (a paraphrase or summary) in column 3. Slowing down to observe the text will help you catch each part of their conversation.

Verses	Moses' Opposition	God's Response
3:11–12	*"Who am I that I should go to Pharoah and bring the children of Israel out of Egypt?"*	*"But I will be with you, and this shall be the sign for you, that I have sent you: when you have brought the people out of Egypt, you shall serve God on this mountain."*
3:13–14		
4:1–9		
4:10–12		
4:13–17		

1. _____

   What do you think was behind Moses' questions and opposition to God's call for him?

2. _____

   How does God react to Moses' questions and opposition?

3. _____

   Which of Moses' oppositions from the chart do you relate to the most? Why?

4. _____

   What other oppositions or questions do you have for God surrounding your own calling?

5.

What is a principle from today's reading that you can hold with you in times of hesitation to obey God? What discovery from today's study can you focus on?

6.

What practical way can you work to overcome your hesitations and doubts?

Go to God *in Prayer.*

Let's take a moment to lay our hearts before the Lord. Share with God your questions and hesitations. Let Moses' exchange with God give you the confidence to be honest before your Heavenly Father today, to tell Him all that is on your heart and mind. Then, leave space and silence for God to respond. Maybe you will hear Him today, or perhaps He'll feel quiet. Either way, have confidence that He *is* with you and *will be* with you, just as He promised Moses. Write your prayer to Him in the space provided.

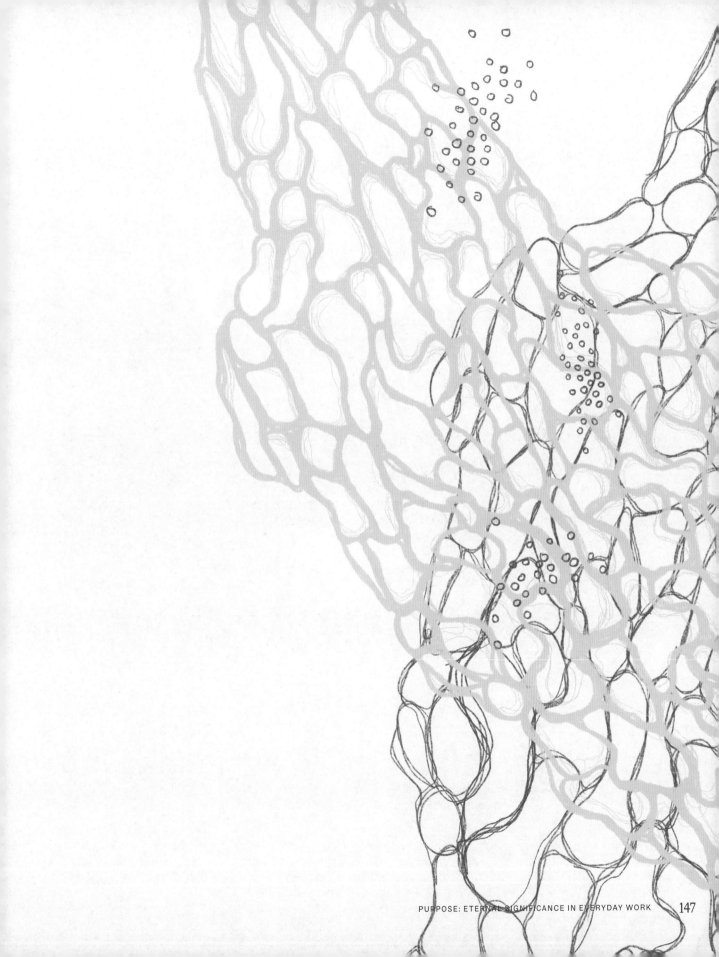

CHAPTER THIRTEEN

Summary

Exodus 3–4

Spend time slowing down and reflecting on all you have discovered from Exodus 3–4 by filling out the chart on the next page. Review previous sessions and all that God has revealed to you.

If you are unable to answer some questions today, that's okay. We will practice this at the end of each passage of Scripture. A question that is hard to answer today may become clearer as you go. At the end of the study, we will look at all the charts together to see the Bible as one full story and how our own stories intersect with God's story.

Theme/Big Idea

What did you learn about God/Jesus?

What did you learn about yourself?

What did you learn about work?

What did you learn about faithful living?

Personal Takeaway

Go to God *in Prayer.*

Let's spend time with God in prayer. Give Him thanks and praise for all He is teaching you and revealing to you about your personal calling. If you have unanswered questions, that's okay. Bring them to God. Sit with Him in any uncertainty that you might be feeling. Tell Him the things that are on your heart. Write your prayer to Him in the space provided.

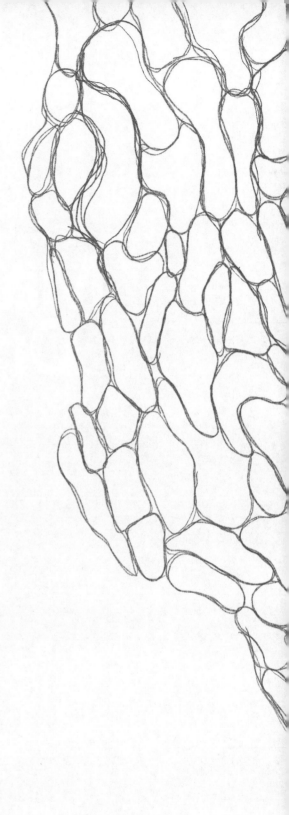

CHAPTER FOURTEEN

Many Gifts, One Spirit

1 Corinthians 12

Now that we have looked at calling, let's turn to another important facet of faith and work—giftings.

Let's begin by reading 1 Corinthians 12.

As you read 1 Corinthians 12, underline each spiritual gift mentioned.

1 Corinthians 12

1 Now concerning spiritual gifts, brothers, I do not want you to be uninformed.

2 You know that when you were pagans you were led astray to mute idols, however you were led.

3 Therefore I want you to understand that no one speaking in the Spirit of God ever says "Jesus is accursed!" and no one can say "Jesus is Lord" except in the Holy Spirit.

4 Now there are varieties of gifts, but the same Spirit;

5 and there are varieties of service, but the same Lord;

6 and there are varieties of activities, but it is the same God who empowers them all in everyone.

7 To each is given the manifestation of the Spirit for the common good.

8 For to one is given through the Spirit the utterance of wisdom, and to another the utterance of knowledge according to the same Spirit,

9 to another faith by the same Spirit, to another gifts of healing by the one Spirit,

10 to another the working of miracles, to another prophecy, to another the ability to distinguish between spirits, to another various kinds of tongues, to another the interpretation of tongues.

11 All these are empowered by one and the same Spirit, who apportions to each one individually as he wills.

12 For just as the body is one and has many members, and all the members of the body, though many, are one body, so it is with Christ.

13 For in one Spirit we were all baptized into one body—Jews or Greeks, slaves or free—and all were made to drink of one Spirit.

14 For the body does not consist of one member but of many.

15 If the foot should say, "Because I am not a hand, I do not belong to the body," that would not make it any less a part of the body.

16 And if the ear should say, "Because I am not an eye, I do not belong to the body," that would not make it any less a part of the body.

17 If the whole body were an eye, where would be the sense of hearing? If the whole body were an ear, where would be the sense of smell?

18 But as it is, God arranged the members in the body, each one of them, as he chose.

19 If all were a single member, where would the body be?

20 As it is, there are many parts, yet one body.

21 The eye cannot say to the hand, "I have no need of you," nor again the head to the feet, "I have no need of you."

22 On the contrary, the parts of the body that seem to be weaker are indispensable,

23 and on those parts of the body that we think less honorable we bestow the greater honor, and our unpresentable parts are treated with greater modesty,

24 which our more presentable parts do not require. But God has so composed the body, giving greater honor to the part that lacked it,

25 that there may be no division in the body, but that the members may have the same care for one another.

26 If one member suffers, all suffer together; if one member is honored, all rejoice together.

27 Now you are the body of Christ and individually members of it.

28 And God has appointed in the church first apostles, second prophets, third teachers, then miracles, then gifts of healing, helping, administrating, and various kinds of tongues.

29 Are all apostles? Are all prophets? Are all teachers? Do all work miracles?

30 Do all possess gifts of healing? Do all speak with tongues? Do all interpret?

31 But earnestly desire the higher gifts.
And I will show you a still more excellent way.

In verses 8–10 and 28, Paul lists several gifts from the Spirit. List these below in column 1. (If a gift is repeated on two lists, record it just once.)

1 Corinthians 12:8–10, 28	Romans 12:6–8	Ephesians 4:11–12
wisdom	*service*	*evangelists*

Then, to round out this list, let's also look at Romans 12:6–8 and Ephesians 4:11–12. Once again, underline any spiritual gifts that are mentioned. List the gifts you see in these verses in its respective column on the chart above. (Again, some gifts will be repeated, but you only need to record it once.)

Romans 12:6–8

6 Having gifts that differ according to the grace given to us, let us use them: if prophecy, in proportion to our faith;

7 if service, in our serving; the one who teaches, in his teaching;

8 the one who exhorts, in his exhortation; the one who contributes, in generosity; the one who leads, with zeal; the one who does acts of mercy, with cheerfulness.

Ephesians 4:11–12

11 And he gave the apostles, the prophets, the evangelists, the shepherds and teachers,

12 to equip the saints for the work of ministry, for building up the body of Christ,

Reflect *and apply.*

As you reflect on the following questions, note that we will talk about both spiritual and natural giftings. The spiritual gifts we observed above are given to us as believers from the Holy Spirit, whereas natural gifts and talents can be inherited and developed. But both are gifts from God and can be used for His glory.

1.

As you look at your lists on the chart, which spiritual gift(s) do you most relate to?
If you are having a hard time figuring it out, ask someone close to you which of these gifts they see in you.

2.

Beyond this list, are there any other gifts that you believe the Lord has given you?
Perhaps natural giftings or talents you inherited or developed?
Again, feel free to ask someone else!

3.

As you look at your current work, where do you see yourself working within these giftings? Where are you not?

4.

How would you like to incorporate these gifts more into your life and work?

5.

What might change if you fully allowed your giftings to inform your work and all you do?

Let's look at key words.

Marking key words in the Bible helps us to slow down and notice patterns and themes that emerge in the text. Look back to 1 Corinthians 12:1–11. Mark the word *Spirit* with a cloud. *Example:* "Now there are varieties of gifts, but the same Spirit"

1. ───────────────────────────────

Who gives us these gifts? Why is this significant?

2. ───────────────────────────────

Looking at verse 7, why are these gifts given to us?

3. ───────────────────────────────

In what ways can your gifts, which you listed on the previous pages, be used in this way?

4.

What is one practical step you could take this week to seek opportunities to use your gifts "for the common good"?

5.

Look to verses 4–6. These three verses have a pattern. In each one, Paul writes, ". . . there are _____, but the same _____." List these three statements below:

- verse 4:

- verse 5:

- verse 6:

6.

In your own words, what is Paul's message for us in these verses? *Note: We will dive deeper into this topic in the next session.*

Go to God *in Prayer.*

Let's take a moment to offer our hearts up to God. Thank Him for the gifts He has graciously and generously given to you. Ask Him to help you look for opportunities to continue to use your gifts for the common good. Lay before Him anything that is on your mind. Write your prayer to God in the space provided.

CHAPTER FIFTEEN

Many Members, One Body

1 Corinthians 12

Let's dive back into 1 Corinthians 12 and take a closer look at verses 12–31.

Reread 1 Corinthians 12.

As you reread 1 Corinthians 12, take note of anything that may be jumping out at you today.

1 Corinthians 12

1   Now concerning spiritual gifts, brothers, I do not want you to be uninformed.

2   You know that when you were pagans you were led astray to mute idols, however you were led.

3   Therefore I want you to understand that no one speaking in the Spirit of God ever says "Jesus is accursed!" and no one can say "Jesus is Lord" except in the Holy Spirit.

4   Now there are varieties of gifts, but the same Spirit;

5   and there are varieties of service, but the same Lord;

6   and there are varieties of activities, but it is the same God who empowers them all in everyone.

7   To each is given the manifestation of the Spirit for the common good.

8   For to one is given through the Spirit the utterance of wisdom, and to another the utterance of knowledge according to the same Spirit,

9   to another faith by the same Spirit, to another gifts of healing by the one Spirit,

10 to another the working of miracles, to another prophecy, to another the ability to distinguish between spirits, to another various kinds of tongues, to another the interpretation of tongues.

11 All these are empowered by one and the same Spirit, who apportions to each one individually as he wills.

12 For just as the body is one and has many members, and all the members of the body, though many, are one body, so it is with Christ.

13 For in one Spirit we were all baptized into one body—Jews or Greeks, slaves or free—and all were made to drink of one Spirit.

14 For the body does not consist of one member but of many.

15 If the foot should say, "Because I am not a hand, I do not belong to the body," that would not make it any less a part of the body.

16 And if the ear should say, "Because I am not an eye, I do not belong to the body," that would not make it any less a part of the body.

17 If the whole body were an eye, where would be the sense of hearing? If the whole body were an ear, where would be the sense of smell?

18 But as it is, God arranged the members in the body, each one of them, as he chose.

19 If all were a single member, where would the body be?

20 As it is, there are many parts, yet one body.

21 The eye cannot say to the hand, "I have no need of you," nor again the head to the feet, "I have no need of you."

22 On the contrary, the parts of the body that seem to be weaker are indispensable,

23 and on those parts of the body that we think less honorable we bestow the greater honor, and our unpresentable parts are treated with greater modesty,

24 which our more presentable parts do not require. But God has so composed the body, giving greater honor to the part that lacked it,

25 that there may be no division in the body, but that the members may have the same care for one another.

26 If one member suffers, all suffer together; if one member is honored, all rejoice together.

27 Now you are the body of Christ and individually members of it.

28 And God has appointed in the church first apostles, second prophets, third teachers, then miracles, then gifts of healing, helping, administrating, and various kinds of tongues.

29 Are all apostles? Are all prophets? Are all teachers? Do all work miracles?

30 Do all possess gifts of healing? Do all speak with tongues? Do all interpret?

31 But earnestly desire the higher gifts.
And I will show you a still more excellent way.

Let's focus on 1 Corinthians 12:12–31.

1.

In verse 12, Paul begins an extended metaphor. What is he comparing the physical human body and its members to?

Paul makes several points within this metaphor. Let's try to understand each one.

2.

For each set of verses below, write what Paul is saying in your own words:

- verses 15–16:

- verses 17–20:

- verses 21–26:

3.

In which of these areas do you feel you struggle the most?

4.

How have you seen all parts of the body needing each other and working well together?

5.

How is this message related to the rest of the chapter we've studied—Paul's teaching on gifts?

6.

In what ways do you find yourself comparing yourself to others, especially when it comes to gifts, calling, or work?

7.

What truth from today's reading can you carry with you to combat those thoughts and feelings of comparison?

Live it out.

Write this truth down and put it where you will see it when you are most tempted to compare yourself to others. Place a sticky note on your work laptop, a widget on your phone, or a note in your desk drawer. Make this a daily reminder that you are a unique and special member of the body, and your gifts are needed.

Go to God *in Prayer.*

Let's end our time today before the Lord. Thank Him for the unique and special ways He has gifted you and that you are a unique and special member of His Body. Confess to Him the times when you did not believe this truth for yourself or for others. Ask for His help and His grace as you journey on. Write your prayer to God in the space provided.

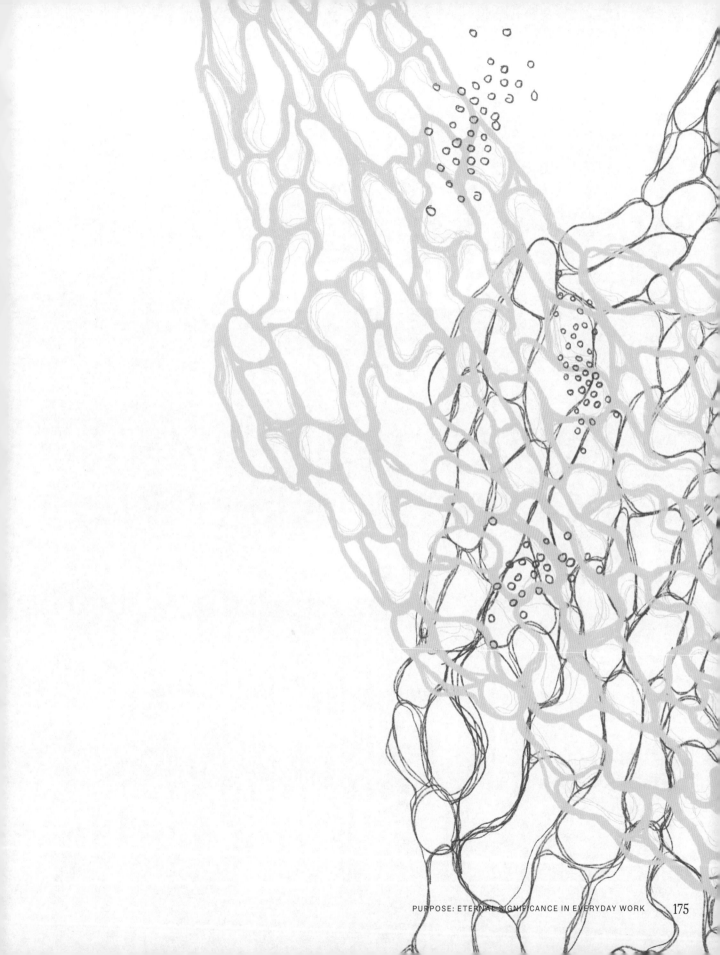

CHAPTER SIXTEEN

Summary

1 Corinthians 12

Spend time slowing down and reflecting on all you have discovered from 1 Corinthians 12 by filling out the chart on the next page. Review previous sessions and all that God has revealed to you.

If you are unable to answer some questions today, that's okay. We will practice this at the end of each passage of Scripture. A question that is hard to answer today may become clearer as you go. At the end of the study, we will look at all the charts together to see the Bible as one full story and how our own stories intersect with God's story.

Theme/Big Idea

What did you learn about God/Jesus?

What did you learn about yourself?

What did you learn about work?

What did you learn about faithful living?

Personal Takeaway

Go to God *in Prayer.*

Let's come before God in prayer. Thank Him for all He has shown you about the unique and special ways He has gifted you. Share with Him the ways you hope to share those gifts with others. Ask Him for the help you need. Write your prayer to God below.

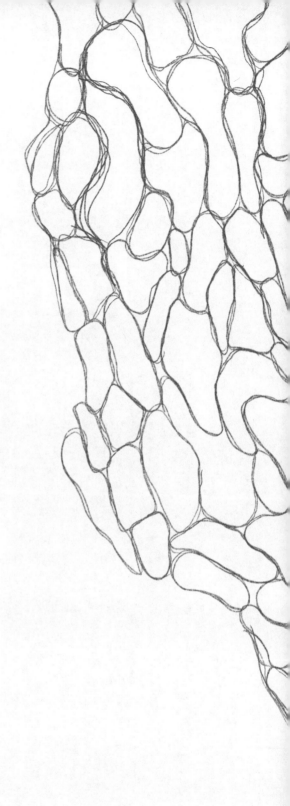

CHAPTER SEVENTEEN

For the Glory

Colossians 3

We have talked about different aspects of faith and work throughout this study. But one question remains: *What's it all for?*

Let's read Colossians 3.

Read through this passage slowly. As you do, take in all of Paul's message.

Colossians 3

1   If then you have been raised with Christ, seek the things that are above, where Christ is, seated at the right hand of God.

2   Set your minds on things that are above, not on things that are on earth.

3   For you have died, and your life is hidden with Christ in God.

4   When Christ who is your life appears, then you also will appear with him in glory.

5   Put to death therefore what is earthly in you: sexual immorality, impurity, passion, evil desire, and covetousness, which is idolatry.

6   On account of these the wrath of God is coming.

7   In these you too once walked, when you were living in them.

8   But now you must put them all away: anger, wrath, malice, slander, and obscene talk from your mouth.

9   Do not lie to one another, seeing that you have put off the old self with its practices

10   and have put on the new self, which is being renewed in knowledge after the image of its creator.

11   Here there is not Greek and Jew, circumcised and uncircumcised, barbarian, Scythian, slave, free; but Christ is all, and in all.

12   Put on then, as God's chosen ones, holy and beloved, compassionate hearts, kindness, humility, meekness, and patience,

13   bearing with one another and, if one has a complaint against another, forgiving each other; as the Lord has forgiven you, so you also must forgive.

14   And above all these put on love, which binds everything together in perfect harmony.

15   And let the peace of Christ rule in your hearts, to which indeed you were called in one body. And be thankful.

16 Let the word of Christ dwell in you richly, teaching and admonishing one another in all wisdom, singing psalms and hymns and spiritual songs, with thankfulness in your hearts to God.

17 And whatever you do, in word or deed, do everything in the name of the Lord Jesus, giving thanks to God the Father through him.

18 Wives, submit to your husbands, as is fitting in the Lord.

19 Husbands, love your wives, and do not be harsh with them.

20 Children, obey your parents in everything, for this pleases the Lord.

21 Fathers, do not provoke your children, lest they become discouraged.

22 Bondservants, obey in everything those who are your earthly masters, not by way of eye-service, as people-pleasers, but with sincerity of heart, fearing the Lord.

23 Whatever you do, work heartily, as for the Lord and not for men,

24 knowing that from the Lord you will receive the inheritance as your reward. You are serving the Lord Christ.

25 For the wrongdoer will be paid back for the wrong he has done, and there is no partiality.

Let's focus on Colossians 3:1–16.

1. ⸻⸻⸻⸻⸻⸻⸻⸻⸻⸻⸻⸻⸻

Make note of anything that immediately stands out to you below.

2. ⸻⸻⸻⸻⸻⸻⸻⸻⸻⸻⸻⸻⸻

2. In verses 1 and 2, Paul gives two clear instructions. Write them below:

- verse 1:

- verse 2:

3. ⸻⸻⸻⸻⸻⸻⸻⸻⸻⸻⸻⸻⸻

In light of all we have learned about faithful living, particularly in *Sojourn,* Part One of our Faithful Living study, what do you think Paul means by these instructions?

4. ───

What is the importance of practicing this today?

Whether we have coworkers, managers, employees, clients, children, or families—work involves other people and relationships. Let's look at verses 8–16.

5. ───

In your work, what difficult relationships exist?

6. ───

Make a list of the things Paul instructs us to put away in verses 8–9:

7.

Make a list of the things Paul instructs us to put on in verses 12–14:

8.

Why is it important that we practice living out these character traits in our work life?

Let's focus on Colossians 3:17–25.

Let's continue into verses 17–25. As you read these verses, keep in mind the message of the beginning of the chapter.

1. ———————————————————————————————

   What is Paul's instruction in verse 17?

2. ———————————————————————————————

   What might Paul mean by his instruction to "do everything in the name of the Lord Jesus"?

3. ———————————————————————————————

   What is Paul's instruction in verses 23–24?

4.

What is Paul's instruction *not* to do?

5.

In what ways do you find yourself struggling to apply this instruction in your own life and work?

6.

In verses 23–24, why does Paul say we should "work heartily as for the Lord . . ."?

7. ———————————————————————————————

What would it look like for you to apply these instructions to your daily work?

8. ———————————————————————————————

In light of today's reading, what is the purpose of your work?

THE GLORY OF GOD

Scan the QR code to learn more about the glory of God in Scripture.

Go to God *in Prayer.*

As we close out our last chapter of this session, let's bring all that is on our hearts and minds before the Lord. Come to Him in thanksgiving. Ask Him to open your eyes, mind, heart, mouth, and hands to bring Him glory through your work today. Ask God to give you the grace to respond to others in love. Write your prayer to Him in the space provided.

CHAPTER EIGHTEEN

Summary

Colossians 3

Spend time slowing down and reflecting on all you have discovered from Colossians 3 by filling out the chart on the next page. Review previous sessions and all that God has revealed to you.

If you are unable to answer some questions today, that's okay. A question that is hard to answer today may become clearer as you go. At the end of the study, we will look at all the charts together to see the Bible as one full story and how our own stories intersect with God's story.

Theme/Big Idea

What did you learn about God/Jesus?

What did you learn about yourself?

What did you learn about work?

What did you learn about faithful living?

Personal Takeaway

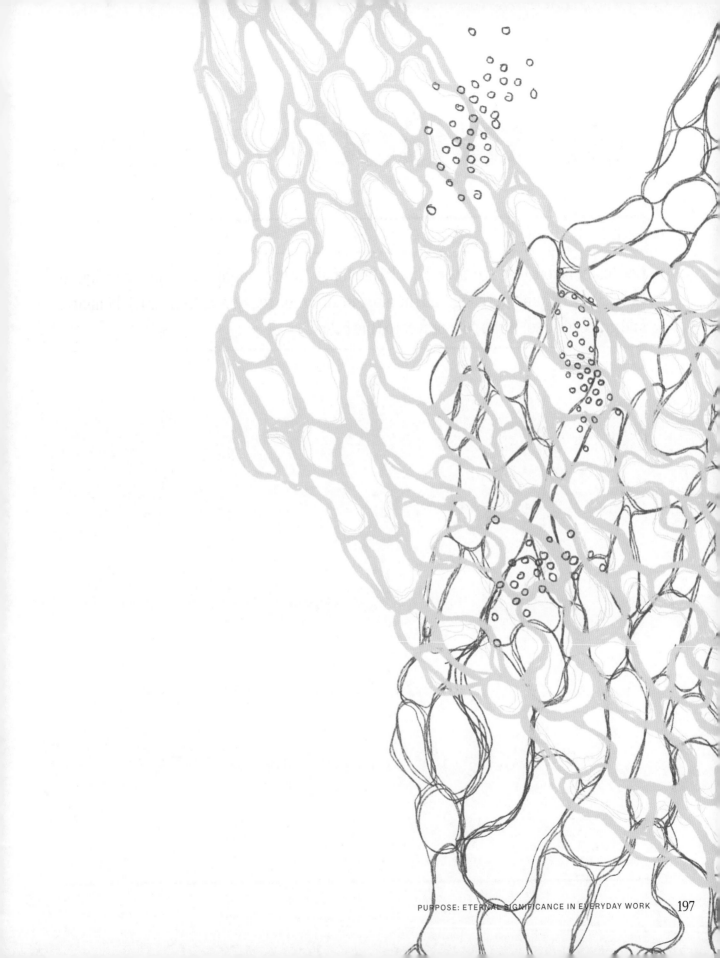

Go to God *in Prayer.*

Let's come before God in prayer. Thank Him for all He has taught you during your time in Colossians. Commit to giving God the glory in all you do today. Ask Him for the humility and grace to do so. Write your prayer to Him below.

CHAPTER NINETEEN

Personal Mission Statement

The final thing we will do together is to write a personal mission statement. Throughout our lives, jobs may change, careers may change, and day-to-day work may change. But our goal in creating a mission statement is to help you, with God's guidance and grace, to discover the mission within you that will not change over your life.

This mission statement will guide you as you move through different career and ministry opportunities. You can filter your work or service decisions through its lens. You can ask yourself, *How can I accomplish my mission through the work I am presently doing?*

Go to God *in Prayer.*

Before we begin, invite God, our Heavenly Father, into this process. We want to approach this in close intimacy with Him, for it is *from* Him and *for* Him that our missions exist. After praying, continue below, remembering to invite Him into every step.

Creating your personal mission statement

Your personal mission statement will answer three questions:

1. *What* do you do?

2. *Who* do you do it for?

3. *How* do you do it?

Let's look at Precept's mission statement as an example. Precept's mission is:

To engage people in relationship with God through knowing His Word.

Now let's look at this mission through the framework of our questions above:

1. *What* do you do?—**Engage people in relationship with God**

2. *Who* do you do it for?—**All people**

3. *How* do you do it?—**Through knowing God's Word**

Let's reflect and pray about these questions one at a time. Keep your answers general in nature.

QUESTION ONE:

What do you do?

This is your *verb*. The thing that God uniquely created you *to do.* Do you serve, teach, communicate, help, create, engage, or cultivate?

If you're feeling stuck:

- Look back to your sections on calling and gifts to help you get started.

- Think through the jobs you've had or places you've served and volunteered—is there a common theme between the ones you enjoyed or those that felt fulfilling?

- Talk with a trusted friend or mentor.

Spend time reflecting and praying on this question. Then, write your thoughts below.

QUESTION TWO:

Who do you do it for?

This is your *who,* but also your *why.* Who is it all for? Maybe it is for all people. Or perhaps God has given you a special heart for a specific group of people—the hurting, people experiencing homelessness, the vulnerable, the next generation. Whom do you want to serve, love, or impact?

Reflect and pray on this question. Then, write your thoughts below.

QUESTION THREE:

How do you do it?

This is your *vehicle.* How do you do the thing that you do? It could be through building relationships and fostering community. Or maybe through sports, art, music, or food. Or through authenticity and vulnerability. Think of activities you have done in the past when you felt truly in your element— when you felt the Spirit of God working in you and through you.

Reflect and pray on this question. Then, write your thoughts below.

Now, let's put it all together into one sentence. Write a draft of your personal mission statement below, knowing that you can come back to it as you continue to pray, discern, serve, and work throughout your life.

My personal mission statement:

Live it out.

Write down the draft of your mission statement where you can see it daily to remind yourself of the immense, beautiful, and unique purpose for which God has created you. Commit to living your mission out every day through the work of your hands.

CONNECTION IN COMMUNITY

Scan the QR code to listen to a roundtable discussion on living on mission.

CHAPTER TWENTY

Self-
Reflection
#3

As we close out our time in this study on faith and work, let's pause and reflect on our journey.

We have traced this thread of faith and work through the Bible—from Nehemiah's story to God's original plan for work and rest in Genesis, from Moses' story in Exodus to Paul's instructions in 1 Corinthians and Colossians. We discovered the beauty, goodness, and purpose behind work as God intended it, and we committed to accomplishing the work at our hands, whatever it may be, for the glory of God.

Before we close, let's revisit the questions you answered at the beginning of this study one last time. While keeping in mind what you have discovered through this study, answer the questions honestly.

Self-Reflection #3

Circle the phrase that describes what you believe about each statement below. Write the references of any relevant verses from our study next to each question, along with any fresh insights or observations.

1. Work was a part of God's original design for humans.

Strongly Disagree   Disagree   Neither Disagree nor Agree   Agree   Strongly Agree

2. God has uniquely gifted me, and I know the gifts that He has given me.

Strongly Disagree   Disagree   Neither Disagree nor Agree   Agree   Strongly Agree

3. God has placed a unique purpose and calling over my life, and I know what it is.

Strongly Disagree   Disagree   Neither Disagree nor Agree   Agree   Strongly Agree

4. I am living out God's calling over my life.

Strongly Disagree   Disagree   Neither Disagree nor Agree   Agree   Strongly Agree

5. I have a clear sense of what would bring me satisfaction and purpose at work.

Strongly Disagree   Disagree   Neither Disagree nor Agree   Agree   Strongly Agree

6. My work is one of the primary ways I praise and glorify the Lord.

Strongly Disagree   Disagree   Neither Disagree nor Agree   Agree   Strongly Agree

7. My work is one of the primary ways I love and serve others.

Strongly Disagree   Disagree   Neither Disagree nor Agree   Agree   Strongly Agree

8. I desire and feel equipped to make rest a part of my weekly rhythm.

Strongly Disagree   Disagree   Neither Disagree nor Agree   Agree   Strongly Agree

journal your thoughts

Revisit your answers from your other Self-Reflection exercises on pages 24–25 and 107–108. Then, journal on the questions below.

1. Have any of your answers changed? If so, *how* have they changed, and *why?*

2. Are there any areas where you feel a disconnect between what you have discovered in Scripture and what you believe or how you feel? *Please know that these disconnects happen to us all. God's grace helps us on the long journey from head knowledge to heart belief.*

3. What questions do you still have for God as you continue this study?

Journal your thoughts and questions here.

Go to God *in Prayer.*

After reflection, take a moment to pray. Give God thanks and glory for our journey. Praise Him for the ways you have grown in Christ. Thank Him for all you have discovered throughout this study. Ask Him for whatever you need to continue your pursuit of faithful living through the work of your hands.

CHAPTER TWENTY-ONE

Wrap-Up

How It Fits Together

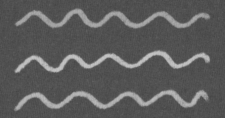

We have journeyed through the Bible in pursuit of faithful living through the work God has given to each one of us—through Nehemiah, Genesis, Exodus, 1 Corinthians, and Colossians. As we wrap up this study, let's take a step back and retrace this thread. Our goal is to understand how the Bible fits together as one full story and to see how our own stories intersect with God's story.

Take some time to review each of the summary charts you filled out, comparing and contrasting them to see the full picture of faithful living in our work throughout Scripture.

Nehemiah 1–2	Page 52
Genesis 1–3	Page 102
Exodus 3–4	Page 150
1 Corinthians 12	Page 178
Colossians 3	Page 196

After you finish, we have a few closing questions.

1. ————————————————————————————————

After tracing the theme of faith and work through these passages of Scripture, how do you understand the Bible to be one whole, continuous story?

2. ————————————————————————————————

How did your understanding of faith and work grow throughout the study?

3. ————————————————————————————————

What are the biggest takeaways you want to remember from this study?

Go to God *in Prayer.*

Come before God and thank Him for being the author of our stories—from the beginning of time until now. Share with Him your feelings and heart as you come to the end of this study. Ask Him to help you remember the truths that you've learned. Invite Him into the rest of your day and your work as you continue to meditate on all you've discovered. Write your prayer to God in the space provided.

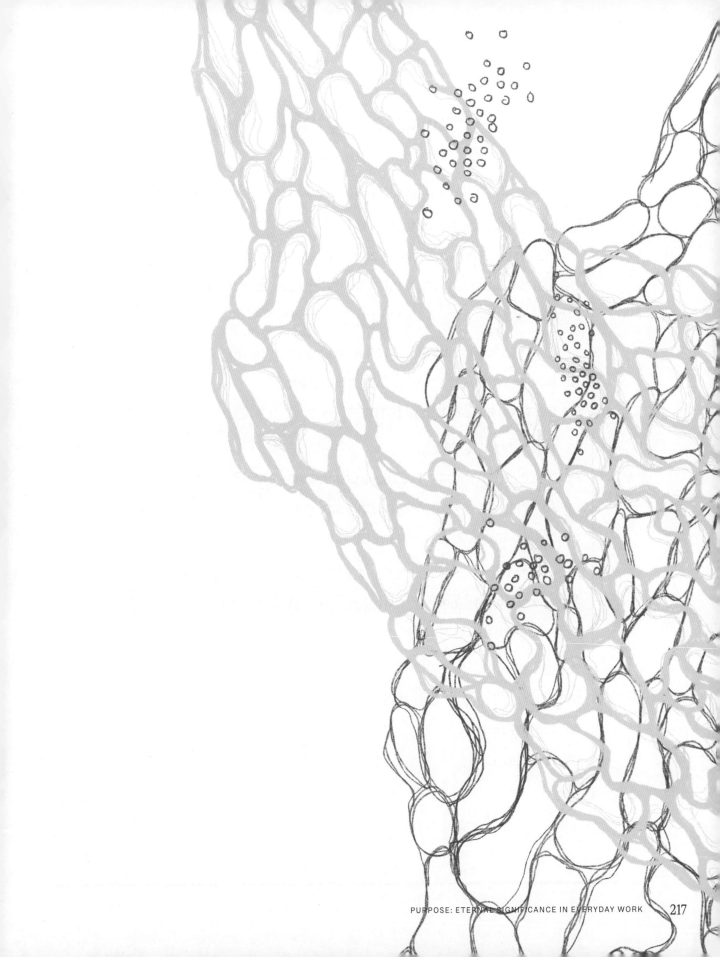

A Prayer for Faithful Living

Good and gracious God from whom all good things flow,

Thank You for the gift of work.
Thank You for the work that is at my hands, even today.
Even in the difficulty, the mundane, the challenge of it all,
I thank You.

Thank You for the calling You have placed over my life,
the unique purpose for which You created me,
the gifts You have entrusted to me.

In all the work I do today,
may I seek to love and serve those around me—
my supervisors, my coworkers, my employees,
my clients, my children, and my family.

May I strive for excellence in the work that is mine to do.
May I work with diligence, patience, humility, kindness, and compassion.
May I seek to live faithfully.

And above all,
May I do it all in Your holy name,
with all my heart,
for Your glory.

Amen.

Letter to the Reader

Thank you for persevering to the end of this study! You made sacrifices, overcame barriers, and chose to come back day after day to sit with the Lord and grow in Christ. You showed up. And you kept showing up. There is truly nothing more important than that.

Through this study, you have seen the beauty and goodness of work. And along the way, you have unearthed bits and pieces of your purpose, calling, and giftings, with which you can love and serve others for the glory of God.

If you have reached the end of this study and still have questions, that's okay. We hope you now have some tools and truths to lean on and come back to as you continue your lifelong pursuit of faithful living. We also hope you have found some community through this process and know that you don't have to do it alone. Most importantly, we pray you have encountered the heart of Jesus, who has been with you all along and will continue to be with you, from now until forever. We are praying alongside you on your journey!

God's grace abounds for you. You are loved.

WAY TO GO!

We'd love to congratulate you personally! Scan the QR code for a video of encouragement from a Yarrow team member!

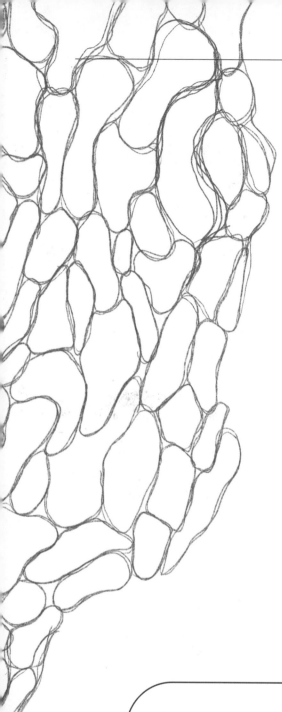

We hope you have enjoyed this Yarrow Bible study guide.

Continue your journey into understanding faithful living in everyday work with the complete Faithful Living Series.

Sojourn:
Flourishing on Earth, Yearning for Heaven
Faithful Living, Part One

Purpose:
Eternal Significance in Everyday Work
Faithful Living, Part Two

Together:
Union with Christ and Each Other
Faithful Living, Part Three

Anchored:
Finding Peace in an Anxious World
Faithful Living, Part Four

Conviction:
Loving Well, Living Differently
Faithful Living, Part Five

For these and other Yarrow Bible Studies, visit Yarrow.org.